TABLE OF CONTENTS

creative ▐➔

— SIDE OUT —

**BE YOURSELF
DO WHAT YOU LOVE
SHARE WHAT YOU DO**

STEVE SAMPLE

Published by Steve Sample Publishing

Cover Design: Dino Marino
Interior Design: Dino Marino

Digital ISBN: 978-1-7338349-1-9
Paperback ISBN: 978-1-7338349-2-6
Hardcover ISBN: 978-1-7338349-3-3

First edition, April 2019

SPECIAL INVITATION
FREE GIFT & LET'S CONNECT

Learn 12 Signs Your Gift is Calling in this FREE Ebook. *Discover Your Gift* is an expansion of Chapter 15 where I provide personal examples of how each sign surfaced on my journey to help me discover my gift and live Creative Side Out:

creativesideout.com/discoveryourgift

You can connect with me personally on Twitter and Instagram @thestevesample. Thank you for allowing me the opportunity to be a part of your journey in life. I look forward to connecting and experiencing your radiance from living Creative Side Out soon!

To my beautiful wife and best friend, Michelle.
For your love, friendship, and sacrifice
that support my dreams.

For my boys Cade, Blake, and Owen.
May you always be yourselves,
do what you love, and share what you do.

INTRODUCTION
A WAY OF LIFE

Creativity is the way I share
my soul with the world.

—Brene Brown

I stood on the street in Nashville. It was early. It was cold. And it was raining. Not pouring, but sprinkling just enough that you could see it in the glow cast from the street lights and watch it disappear into the tree tops with just enough sound to enhance the quiet darkness.

I threw my backpack and guitar in the backseat of my ride to the airport. I took one last look around at the city I had come to love so much. I closed my eyes, breathed in deep, and hung on to the moment giving my soul one last chance to soak it up. As the rain hit my face, I exhaled and opened my eyes. I didn't want to leave, but it was time to go.

Within a few hours my flight touched down in Texas. I made it home in time for the late Sunday service with my family. If I'm being honest though, I wasn't paying much attention to the message. My mind kept replaying the previous four days in Nashville. I couldn't stop thinking about the people I had connected with, the stories we shared, and the songs we wrote. It was satisfying and fulfilling. It was meaningful and important. It was _my_ definition of success.

It's hard to believe, but just a few years ago I wasn't writing at all. For three years I didn't write a single song. Not only had I quit going to Nashville, but I had also quit my career as a real estate professional. I wasn't sure what I was looking for in life. I just knew that I hadn't found whatever it was on either of those paths.

Real estate was the path I saw to success, but crossing milestones and achieving goals in my professional career were not providing me with satisfaction and fulfillment. Songwriting was fun and enjoyable, but I never considered myself a gifted writer. I could only see that my chances of that path leading to success were slim to none. So, I abandoned both paths in my life.

Each day the world continues to move a little faster than it did the day before. It's easy to get caught in the flow of life without giving intentional thought to our purpose and what we want in life. That's what happened to me. I was lost. Something was missing.

Today, I know exactly what I had been missing. Now, I have

found what I was looking for and am walking the one true path in life I was meant to walk. That something missing in my life was significance. Living Creative Side Out is how I found it.

Success was an external force pulling at me before I even realized what it was or the role it played in my life. What little I knew about success is what motivated me to get good grades as a kid and served as my drive to go to college. It impacted what I studied and ultimately influenced my career choice based on the lifestyle I desired.

Little did I know that from a very early age there was a second force at work in my life playing a much different role. It was an internal, more subtle force, yet it was powerful enough to cut through the noise of the outside world and get my attention over and over again throughout the years. It was my natural interest, curiosity, and desire to write. More specifically, it was a draw toward music and a call to write songs.

During my time away from both real estate and writing, I realized the disconnect was not in the two paths I chose to walk, but in what I expected to get from each. I had been making decisions on both paths based on success alone and was ignoring meaning and importance. To make things worse, I wasn't even using my definition of success as a metric. I had been so focused on chasing success when what I was really seeking was significance.

Today, I am a songwriter and an author. I finally found fulfillment and satisfaction in my life once I discovered, embraced, and committed to pursuing my purpose as a storyteller. However, I lived life for far too long with a constant tension between the competing ideas of chasing success and pursuing significance.

Once I realized that success was useless in my life if it wasn't rooted in meaning and importance, I had discovered a new way to live my life. I started taking my inner creativity, natural interest, and curiosity which had meaning and importance to me and started using it to identify the external tasks, milestones, and goals that would provide me the satisfaction and fulfillment that I was seeking in life.

I began living Creative Side Out, which simply means being ourselves, doing what we love, and sharing what we do. Our natural interest, curiosity, and desire to learn, explore, and play toward a subject is our inner creativity. It's who we are at our very core. When we discover that authenticity and allow ourselves the time, energy, and attention to engage that inner creativity, we can use it, grow it, and share it in the outside world. We can live Creative Side Out; we can live the life we are called to live, meant to live, and deserve to live.

So, if my struggles sound familiar, this book is for you. Creative Side Out is my story of finding the one true authentic path I was meant to walk in life. You can apply the lessons I learned in your life to help you do the same. There are several forces at play in our lives. We have to be aware of those forces and the roles they play to navigate our lives to find our genuine path and stay on it.

If you commit to taking the journey page by page and fully engaging in the exercises, you will understand what's missing in your life, have a clear direction moving forward, and develop a plan for crossing the milestones and achieving the goals that will bring meaning and importance to your life. In other words, you will have discovered your own personal path to finding significance in your life.

When we encounter others living a significant life, they radiate. We are drawn to them. They are helpful, happy, and contagious. We know when we are in the presence of someone living Creative Side Out. We may not be able to put our finger on just what it is that attracts us to them. However, we know that whatever they have in their life that makes them radiate, we want it.

Don't continue life wishing you had that radiance. Don't keep living life without direction or with that something's missing feeling. You can have what they have. You can be the person that everyone else encounters with that radiance living a life of significance.

Congratulations on taking the first step toward living Creative Side Out by opening this book. Reading it will help you find your path and take the journey you are called to take. However, the book is designed to have the maximum results if you schedule the time to put thought into the exercises and dig deep to answer the questions.

For your convenience, a companion workbook is available for you to use as you make progress on your journey through the book. However, a pen and a journal will work just as well. Making the decision and commitment to be yourself, do what you love, and share what you do is what's most important.

There's one last thing before we get started. To be clear, I haven't made it in the music business. No major artists have recorded my songs. None of the songs I have written have made the radio, won any awards, or even been nominated. I have never placed a song in a film or on a television show, or even a commercial. To date, I have not made a single dollar off of a song that I have written.

However, I am just like you. I am an everyday person with a limited amount of time each day. I still have a day job. I have a family and other day-to-day life responsibilities. Yet, I am focused on becoming an established writer and am making progress toward my goal. I have learned to embrace the journey, soak up little victories and use them to propel me forward on this path, and am having success.

As I reflect back on my trip to Nashville, I am amazed at how far I have come with my writing. I continue to write better songs, and make more and more genuine connections with some of the best writers in the world along with other industry professionals. There is no doubt in my mind that I am on the right path, doing what I was meant to do in this life, being the person I was created to be, and doing the work I am being called to do.

We all have to start somewhere on our journey. None of us start out as professionals. We all start out awkward and unsure. However, if we just start and develop a plan for growth, we will gain momentum, and we will become skilled and confident in our abilities.

The only thing we need to take that first step is a natural interest, curiosity, and desire. If you don't know what that is for you, I can help you discover it, use it, grow it, and share it to help you find success rooted in significance on your one true path in life.

If living life to the fullest while maximizing your impact on the world sounds like the life you want to discover and explore, then let's get started. The illustration below represents us in motion on our path in life. The circle is us, and the arrow is our path. With that said, let our journey begin.

This is us living life...

CHAPTER 1

SUCCESS

Success: Your definition will determine your destination. It should be a destination at which you want to arrive.

—Victoria S. Carlson

I had a pretty normal childhood. I grew up in a true middle class neighborhood, not an upper middle class neighborhood. In fact, the longer we lived there the more it slipped toward a lower middle class neighborhood.

When I was in the fifth grade, there were two stabbings at the junior high I was supposed to attend for sixth grade. So, my parents enrolled me in Catholic school. My parents didn't have the money to send me to private school, but they found a way. I was there, I was safe, and I definitely got a better education than the alternative. However, it didn't take me long to realize that many of the kids came from much more affluent environments than I did.

There were a lot of kids like me in private school. Their parents were scraping by to provide the best environments they possibly could for their kids. However, there was also quite a bit of wealth. Many of my classmates lived in bigger houses than I did. Their parents drove newer, more luxurious vehicles. They took vacations that required them to get on an airplane and fly. Some of them were even flying to second homes that their parents owned in different parts of the world.

It felt like I was living two different lives. I had school and that set of friends. Then I would come home and play in the evenings and weekends with my neighborhood friends. I had well-off friends. I had middle class friends. And I had friends that, quite honestly, were poor.

So, when my friends at school started comparing SAT scores and discussing which colleges they were applying to, I realized that none of my neighborhood friends and I had ever even discussed it.

I always assumed I would go to college, but never gave it much thought. I knew I wanted to buy houses like my school friends lived in. I knew I wanted nice cars like their parents drove. I knew I wanted to be more comfortable financially than everyone in the neighborhood I grew up in including my parents.

I had no clue how to apply to college or which one I wanted to attend. I had no idea what I wanted to do in life. I didn't give much thought as to how I was going to do it, but the one thing I knew for sure, 100 percent, without a doubt, was that I wanted to be successful.

ACHIEVING OUR GOALS

Success was a force in my life long before I realized it was at work. Let's take a deeper look at how our path in life is influenced by success and the role it plays in our lives.

By definition, success is the favorable attempt of endeavors. It is simply achieving a desired outcome. We set a goal. We identify the major milestones to get us from our current reality to our goal. Then we identify the tasks required between each milestone to keep us progressing toward our goal.

We make up our mind, set a goal, and start crossing off tasks one by one. We check off each of the milestones as we surpass them, and eventually we achieve our goal. We succeed.

EXTERNAL & MEASURABLE

Our path to success is external. We physically do things in our pursuit of success. There are outward signs of success. We can see if someone has completed a task. We can see if they have checked a box and crossed a milestone. We can see if they have achieved their goal.

Success:
Tasks, Milestones & Goals

(External)

The outside world can see if we are successful in our endeavors. We see each other engaged in tasks at school for a grade. We see each other pass our classes and move on to the next grade level. We see who graduates and who does not. When we are on the path to success it is measurable.

KEEPING SCORE

If we can measure it, we can compare it. It's human nature to compare ourselves to those around us. From an early age, we learn that we live in a very competitive world.

Possessions, sports, and academics fill our childhood experiences. We naturally begin to evaluate where we stand among those around us. We compare our team's record against those of other teams. We track our personal performance and we measure it against our teammates. We compare our grades to those of our friends.

If we are motivated by competition in the slightest, we constantly check the world around us in everything we do to find the established benchmark. We then make adjustments and immediately pursue beating the mark established by others.

OUTSIDE INFLUENCE

Growing up, my competitive nature and encouragement from others pushed me to keep up and motivated me to surpass those around me. My reality, definitions, and perceptions were comprised of bits and pieces of everyone else's world around me.

My definition of success began to look a lot like everyone else's definition around me. My path became heavily influenced by what my friends were doing, what I perceived my parents wanted me to do, and what I absorbed through media and pop culture. When you reflect on your school years, does your experience sound like mine?

The world around us is heading in a general direction. That world moves fast, and we fear being left behind. So, we don't give it much thought. Whether we realize it or not, the environment around us and the world we grew up in has defined success for us and set us in motion on a path to achieve it.

CREATIVE SIDE OUT HANDBOOK

1. Success is the result of completing tasks and crossing milestones to achieve a goal.

2. Those tasks, milestones, and goals are external accom-

plishments that can be measured and observed by others.

3. Our competitive human nature drives us to set goals similar to those around us and keep score to compare our level of success to that of others.

DISCOVER & EXPLORE YOUR PATH

1. List the goals you are currently pursuing. Then list the goals you would like to pursue. What are the external signs of success that others will see if you accomplish these goals? Who or what influenced you to want to set these goals and pursue them? Do you know others pursuing any of these goals you listed? If so, do you discuss who's winning with them or secretly keep score? Who do you update on your progress and compare notes with on a regular basis?

2. What is your definition of success? Write down what immediately comes to mind without much reflection. Identify your influences that have impacted and helped you shape the definition of success that you just wrote down.

3. What will success in your achievement of these goals mean to you? How important are they to you on a scale of one to ten with one having no importance in your life and ten having extreme importance in your life? Are these goals truly what you want for yourself?

MORE TO THE STORY

Like most kids, I lived in the moment. Without even being aware, my external environment and outside influences shaped my perception of the world. I was absorbing differences in social classes, education levels, income, lifestyle, grades, wins, losses, and every other outward sign people use to define success, measure progress, and keep score.

Success was a force pulling at me before I even realized what it was or the role it played in my life. Little did I know that there was a second force at work playing a much different role in my life. It was an internal, more subtle force, yet it was powerful enough to cut through the noise of the outside world and get my attention.

CHAPTER 2
SIGNIFICANCE

Remember, the human heart is on a quest
for happiness; to believe that we can
find happiness without discovering
our essential purpose is foolish.

—Matthew Kelly

When I was a boy, I had a record player with two 45s. My record player eventually gave way to a large boom box in the '80s. My boom box fell from grace one Christmas when Santa brought me a home stereo with dual cassette trays. That stereo became the center of my world for many years.

I made mix tapes of all my favorite songs. If I didn't have a song I wanted to include, I would wait for hours to hear it on the radio and press record to include it in my mix. I would pick up additional home stereo speakers and boxes here and there from friends. I would take them apart, mix and match them, and continually change my setup in search of the best sound for my small bedroom.

I loved music but I didn't realize how much I loved it.

Even as I got older when sports, grades, and friends began to consume the hours of my days, I still made room for music in my life. After perfecting my home stereo system, I became obsessed with perfecting the sound system in my truck.

The mix tape was replaced with compact discs. No one had the ability to burn them yet, so growing my CD collection took most of the cash I ever earned and received. I became a member of two different CD subscription services.

In addition to collecting music, I started to take notice of my friends that could play instruments and sing. I became fascinated with their abilities to play and I decided to buy a used guitar from a friend.

It seemed so complicated. I was intimidated by it. Yet, I so badly wanted to learn to play. I had a natural curiosity that kept driving me to pick up that guitar and try. However, playing it did not come naturally at all. I would get discouraged, frustrated, and disappointed. Many times I would put it down and walk away.

However, I always picked it back up. I had no sense of timing. I couldn't get my fingers to press all of the strings simultaneously. The pick felt uncomfortable in my hands, and I would often drop it while strumming. Guitars were not supposed to make such awful sounds, but I kept making them.

It was bad, and I didn't think I would ever learn how to play the guitar.

When I graduated high school, I still couldn't play well at all, but I wasn't putting the guitar down as often. My natural drive, curiosity, and interest in making music was not fading. I wouldn't recognize it until after college, but music was becoming a significant part of my identity.

OF MEANING & IMPORTANCE

What I didn't know at the time was that my attraction to music and desire to play guitar was a yearning for significance. Like success, significance was also at work in my life before I knew what it was. Let's take a deeper look at the role it plays in our lives.

By definition, significance is qualified as having consequence. Significance is simply having the qualities of meaning and importance.

We seek things and experiences that bring meaning and importance to our lives. We are on a journey to find value in our lives. We can also find meaning and importance by adding value to other people's lives.

INTERNAL & ABSTRACT

We can't easily see significance in others or in the physical world like we can success. Unlike success, significance is internal and abstract. There are no obvious outward signs of it, but we can definitely sense it, both in others and in ourselves.

Significance:

(Internal)

Meaning & Importance

Growing up, I was not exposed to significance like I was to success. Finding importance and meaning was not displayed, measured, and talked about with my friends and my circle of influence like success was. It was not as often taught and encouraged. And it was not as prevalent in the everyday world around me. I've come to believe that the same could be said for most people I know.

We talk to our friends and trade stories with those around us about our achievements. We have a tendency not to discuss what those achievements mean to us or how important they are to us. Meaning and importance tends to be very personal in our lives, and we can be shy about sharing it with others.

NO COMPARISON

We can't measure significance concretely, so we don't compare it like we do success. When we cannot see and measure something, it is abstract, and we have a harder time understanding it.

If we don't completely understand significance in our own lives, we certainly don't understand it in other people's lives. Significance is personal. So, we tend to protect it rather than put it out into the world for comparison.

REFLECTION REQUIRED

The external world and our drive for success keep us moving through life at a very fast pace. It's hard for us to slow down and reflect on the decisions we make.

We can even get caught up making big decisions in life, like changing careers or getting married, based on what the world around us is doing rather than by how much value it will add to our lives.

What is important and means something to us can be very different from that of those around us. Even our closest friends and family with whom we may have a ton in common with see value in different things and experiences than we do.

Our sense of meaning and importance is below the surface and requires that we take the time to reflect internally to discover it. When we take the time to temporarily remove ourselves from the outside world, we can uncover why we pursue what we do and begin to make more conscious decisions in life that support our desire for significance.

CREATIVE SIDE OUT HANDBOOK

1. Significance comes from experiences and interactions that provide meaning and importance.

2. Meaning and importance are abstract and internal so that others cannot easily see and measure significance in our lives unless we reveal our personal feelings.

3. Significance is unique and personal, and it requires internal reflection to discover what is significant for each of us.

DISCOVER & EXPLORE YOUR PATH

1. What activities, subjects, or interests have meaning to you and are important to you in your life? Reflect on a moment when an experience with each of those you listed unlocked an undeniable connection that resonated with you.

2. Can others see your natural draw toward these interests? If not, do you openly share your draw to these activities, subjects, and interests, or do you keep them to yourself for the most part? If you do share these interests with

others, do you share with everyone or just a select group of close friends and family?

3. Take a moment to reflect on these activities, subjects, and interests a bit deeper. Are you naturally drawn to them and curious to learn more on a regular basis? Would you consider these interests to have significance in your life?

MORE TO THE STORY

At first I didn't think much of my attraction to music. I just went with it. I listened to music. I read about music. I played to the best my ability would allow and was eager to learn anything from anyone who was better than me. It got so that I couldn't walk past my guitar without picking it up, whether I had five minutes or a whole day to spend playing. I even practiced when I was already late with no time to spare at all.

Looking back on it now, my attraction to music was more than simply how I avoided boredom. It was intriguing. It engaged my whole mind and being. I was interested and curious in learning all that I could. From my early years, it quietly and steadily became meaningful and important to me. Unknown to me, music was subtly forming the foundation of significance in my life.

CHAPTER 3
FINDING OUR WAY

You have two choices in your life;
you can dissolve into the mainstream,
or you can be distinct.
To be distinct, you must be different.
To be different, you must strive
to be what no one else but you can be.

—Alan Ashley-Pitt

Success was a force working to push me along in the flow of life around me, even before I was aware of it. Meanwhile, my quest for significance pulled at me in a more subtle manner and somewhat against the current of my pursuit of success in life. For many years, success and significance sparred with one another, each urging me to walk a different path as I tried to find my way in life.

SUCCESS

By the time I graduated from high school, my definition of success was formed. I wanted to make a lot of money, live in a big house, have nice things, and take awesome vacations. So, without giving it too much thought, off I went and did what the world around me expected me to do: I went to college.

I still had no idea what I was going to do to become successful. I liked drawing. I liked houses. I thought about going into architecture. However, right or wrong, someone told me that architects didn't make much money.

We had a family friend that I knew to be very successful. He was a stockbroker. Stockbrokers were always wealthy in the movies and on TV. Stockbrokers majored in finance. Finance was in the business school. Almost all of my friends were going into the business school. So, finance it was.

SIGNIFICANCE

It didn't take me long to discover that a college town was fertile ground for finding and growing an interest in music. It started with live music at worship services. Then I found local rock bands in tiny bars. The major concerts rolled into town like Garth Brooks, Clay Walker, and the Dixie Chicks. The pull toward music was growing strong.

When the Texas music revolution caught fire, guys like Robert Earl Keen, Pat Green, Cross Canadian Ragweed, and so many others cast out their lines, hooked my soul, and pulled me hard toward music like a fish toward the boat.

I still couldn't play my guitar very well. I struggled to learn to play covers. Playing and singing with my awful timing and voice was making my future in music look pretty bleak. But I did it anyway.

One night, I started writing a song. It sucked. I sucked. Eventually, with just enough courage at a party one night, I played it. Of all things, my friends said three words that would forever change my life: "Play it again."

This spurred me on. I started always taking my guitar to parties and writing spur of the moment songs to entertain my friends. I'd made a discovery. It was as if a seed had been planted in me. Music naturally continued to grow in my life and my passion had branched into songwriting.

SUCCESS

My junior year I enrolled in Accounting 301 and realized I hated finance. My roommate was in marketing, which appealed to my creative side and was still in the business school. I changed my major and really enjoyed it.

As graduation approached, I decided an ad agency was perfect for me. I liked drawing, art, writing, songs, and jingles. An ad agency sounded like the perfect place to balance my creativity and new-found business knowledge. I toured ad agencies in Houston and Dallas. I loved the environment, atmosphere, people, projects, and overall vibe.

It turns out a lot of marketing majors liked ad agencies. There was fierce competition for open positions, and to break into the business you had to be willing to work for next to nothing. Working for less than half of what my friends were making didn't sound like success to me.

I ended up going to work for a homebuilder. Within a short time I discovered that the homebuilder bought lots from a land developer. Developers apparently made a lot of money. So, again without too much thought, back to grad school I went to learn real estate development, which sent me right back to the finance department.

SIGNIFICANCE

Even though I still was not very good at playing and singing, a friend asked me to come to an open mic night with him. I sucked at playing guitar. I had no rhythm. I couldn't sing. I still struggled to play covers. So, I played original songs that were very linear, way too long, and quite frankly not good. Additionally, I only played them for small groups of friends in a safe environment. I didn't play in public places for people I didn't know and open myself up to ridicule and laughter.

Yet, I went and I played. The open mic scene eventually led to me getting asked to play in a band. We were not very good. We were all still learning our instruments, but we got better. We landed a standing gig and attracted a regular Wednesday night crowd.

In between sets, I would even willingly grab the guitar, sit on a stool by myself without the band and play original songs I had written. One of my songs eventually resonated with people. I started getting requests for it and after shows, people would tell me how much they related to it. My band incorporated it into our set list. Then another band started playing it at their shows.

Hearing others sing my song and watching it connect with an audience opened my eyes. Songwriting was something I could become good at if I worked hard enough. Writing a song that connected so deeply with others gave me a special feeling. I wanted to repeat it. I wanted every song to start connecting with others like that.

So many people spend their entire lives trying to figure out their purpose in life. I had stumbled upon my source of meaning and importance in my journey of life, though I didn't fully recognize it. Even though I didn't fully know the role writing was playing in my life, I started to embrace it.

HEALTHY DISCOVERY

The push and pull of success and significance in my life often felt erratic, messy, and uncharted. In hindsight, I've come to realize it's supposed to feel that way.

As we transition from adolescence to young adult, we gain in-dependence and begin a period of healthy discovery about the world around us and discover options that we didn't even know existed. Every time our circle of friends and influence change, we naturally get exposed to different environments and new experiences.

This is an exciting time in life. We test and try new and different things. We bounce around in the river of life and play.

FINDING BOUNDARIES

This period in our lives, whether we know it or not, is where we explore both the external world of success and the internal world of significance.

Finding our way

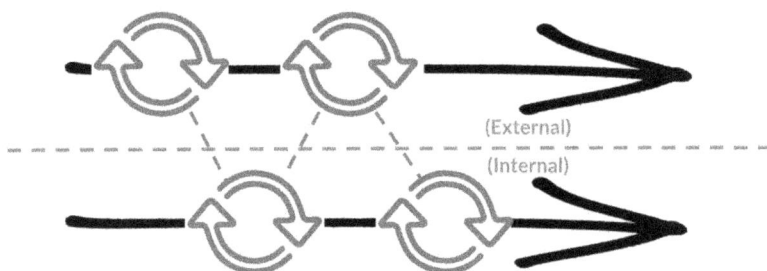

We follow the crowd and we explore our own path. We change crowds now and again, and we continue to explore different internal paths as well. During this time, we most likely don't even realize the role each path is playing in our lives.

We find the boundaries where most people exist and explore success and significance within those boundaries. Inside this "normal range" we don't cause waves, and we don't want to draw too much attention to ourselves. We try to fit in and we go with the flow as we continue healthy discovery.

Normal Range

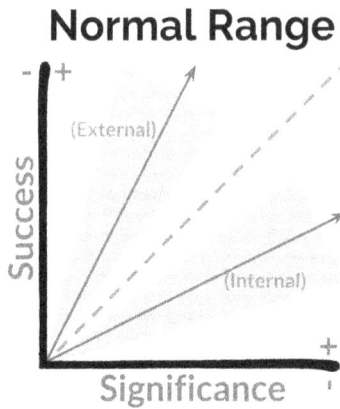

THE CURRENT OF LIFE

When we first jump in the river as young adults and begin to play, we often don't realize that the river has a current. When we go with the flow of the crowd around us on the external path of success, we can find ourselves swept downstream rather quickly and without much control.

On the other hand, when we slow down and try to navigate our internal path of significance, it can often feel like we're swimming against the current. Our path looks and feels different than everyone else's. We don't want to be judged, so we often test swimming upstream in small spurts, hoping no one will notice.

We are surrounded every day in real life and on TV and social media by people enjoying the material gains that we recognize as hallmarks of success. We don't typically encounter a lot of people that gracefully swim against the current. We don't often have role models for how to outwardly pursue significance in our lives.

We fear getting left behind as our circle of friends and influence race further downstream. So, we go with the flow. However, if we are not careful, we can look up in a few years, not recognize where we are, and struggle to get back on course.

We are pulled along by the world around us whether that is the direction we want to go or not. If we have interest in a different direction than the one the world is taking us down, then we have to slow down and pay attention when we feel a call toward that path even if it feels like we are swimming against the current and drawing attention to ourselves. We may even feel like we are being pushed from our comfort zone, but if we spend too much time going with the flow in one direction, it may be difficult to swim back in the direction that we really want to go in life.

CREATIVE SIDE OUT HANDBOOK

1. As young adults finding our way in life, we are exposed to many different circles of friends and influences as we try new things.

2. When we relax in a comfortable environment, we can get caught in that environment's current and go with the flow, floating along between the banks of everyone else's normal boundaries.

3. Slowing down and making sure we are truly pursuing the path we want to take in life can often draw unwanted attention to our path and make us feel like we are swimming against the current of life, but if we don't, we may find it difficult to pursue the most personally satisfying path.

DISCOVER & EXPLORE YOUR PATH

1. What circles of influence are you currently active with on a regular basis? Whether you interact with them daily, once a week, once a month, or only once a year, identify each group that has any current influence in your life. Do the same for any group in the past that had such an influence on you and that may still be having an impact on who you are. Examples of these groups could be family, high school friends, college friends, church groups, industry associates, and so forth.

2. Are there any decisions in life that you have made that these groups have influenced? Would you have made the same decisions if you had not known these groups? In retrospect, were these decisions the right ones? Would you make the same decisions again?

3. Are there any interests in your life now or in the past
   that you have wanted to pursue that would pull you
   against the current of these circles of influence? Has
   your involvement with these circles of influence pre-
   vented you from pursuing any of those interests? Circle
   the interests you have listed that you still want to pursue whether you are currently pursuing them or not.

MORE TO THE STORY

At the age of 25, I graduated from grad school and began a
career in real estate development. Milestone achieved, I was firmly
on a path toward success. I had also discovered my call to music. I
was beginning to realize it was a part of my identity and a source of
meaning and importance in my life.

Little did I know that two opposing forces, success and significance, had quietly taken sides and drawn a line in the sand. They
were about to erupt in a war of massive proportions in my life that
would last for over a decade

CHAPTER 4
FINDING OUR WAR

*When we separate the daily activities of our lives
from our essential purpose, the very meaning of
our lives, it is only a matter of time before
despair and desperation take hold of us.*

—Matthew Kelly

The flow of life in the external world had been pushing me to find a path to success and make as much money as I could. However, the voice that kept calling me to swim against the current toward music had continued to grow and was stronger than ever. Success and significance soon launched an all-out attack in my head, heart, and soul battling for my attention, time, and energy.

SUCCESS FIRED THE FIRST SHOT

A month and a half after grad school, I got married. My wife and I consolidated our student loans and owed just shy of $100,000. That covered three degrees between the two of us, and neither one of us was a doctor or a lawyer.

The band broke up, and I shoved music aside. It was time to go to work. The real world with all its responsibilities had presented itself in full force. Music was simply a hobby, and I still wasn't all that great at it anyway.

I had landed a job with a real estate developer, and I was excited to learn the business. I immediately submersed myself in my career. I envisioned myself in a corner office one day. I was driven by success as defined by the new world around me.

As I became more entrenched in the world of real estate developers and met more people in the industry, my definition of success began to look a lot like that of those at the top of the industry. Success included a million dollar home, extravagant things, and a supreme level of financial freedom and comfort for myself and my family.

SIGNIFICANCE RESPONDED

Entrenched as I was in my career, it remained difficult for me to come home and walk past a guitar without picking it up. I would get lost playing, and an hour or two would fly by. I started writing again sporadically as bits and pieces would pop into my head.

A passion for songwriting grew inside of me. I read books about songwriting and the craft. I began soaking up any publication or interview I could find with songwriters talking about writing and their process. I developed a hunger to learn the story behind every song. I wanted to know the complete journey of every song I liked from idea to finished song to demo to pitch to recording and how it made its way to being a radio single.

Then I did a very dangerous thing: I started dreaming. I dreamed about Nashville and what it would be like to get a song on the radio. Before I knew it, the extra energy and time that I once spent learning everything I could about real estate development was overtaken with all things songwriting.

I started spending time away from work playing, learning, and dreaming rather than reading, learning, and networking for my career. While all of my friends spent their spare time trying to figure out how to advance their profession, I daydreamed, wrote, and researched writing and Nashville. For the most part, I kept this obsession to myself out of fear of what others would think.

SUCCESS FOUND ALLIES

My circle of friends and influence was comprised entirely of friends from college and my growing network of real estate professionals. I spent my days hanging out with ambitious young real estate professionals and seasoned real estate titans at the top of their game. I spent evenings and weekends with my friends from college who were all focused on advancing their careers in their respective fields and well on their way to success.

I didn't harbor the same ambitions as they did-at least not toward my real estate career. This weighed heavily on me. I felt guilty. I felt like a failure. I was letting my family down. Songwriting was child's play and getting in the way of my success.

So, I walked away from my writing. Fear of getting left behind by the world around me drove me to go all in on the external path of success. This meant taking the time that I used to spend writing to now focusing on real estate, my projects, the industry, and networking more than I had in the past.

SIGNIFICANCE GREW ITS FORCES

No matter how many times I gave up pursuing music's call, I kept getting drawn back into it. It wouldn't take much ... the beat of the kick drum in my chest at a live show, a new song on the radio, an interview with a writer or artist, or simply picking up my guitar and playing it. Just like that, I was back, and each time the pull toward music was stronger than before.

This natural connection to music was growing to the point that I had to share it with others. I discovered local song circles and started attending monthly guitar pulls and song swaps. I met other people who, like me, were addicted to playing and writing. Real estate development paid the bills but writing songs and playing for small crowds of like-minded creatives brought meaning and importance to my life.

Other writers invited friends, family and co-workers to the song circles to hear them play. Not me. There was no way I was going to take the chance that someone I knew didn't get it or thought that I sucked. I feared what they might think, and I protected my source of meaning and importance from judgment at all costs.

SUCCESS DROPPED A BOMB

Three years into our marriage, my wife gave birth to our first child. In an instant, priorities and responsibilities changed. Two years later we were blessed with another son. The cost of child care versus my wife's teaching salary was almost a wash. So, we decided we would rather her stay at home and raise our kids.

The obligation to provide for my family grew exponentially as a result of that decision. It was time to really get serious about advancing my career, climbing the ladder, and achieving financial success.

Again, I shoved music aside like a branch blocking the path I was walking. I threw myself to the extreme side of success pouring myself into my work and trying to catch up with my industry peers. I was once again determined to make as much money as I could for my family and provide us all with a level of comfort far beyond what we had.

SIGNIFICANCE ROSE FROM THE ASHES

The obligation to provide for my family weighed heavily on me. However, the thought of not teaching my boys to pursue the life they were meant to live with all of their being was even more powerful. The only way to do that was by example.

The clock was ticking. I knew the chaos of family life would come full force in a few years as our boys began to walk, run, ride bikes, and play, and they would need me fully present in their lives. If I was ever going to chase the dream a little harder, I needed to do it right then, while they were little. I knew exactly what I had to do. It was time to visit Nashville.

I spent the flight there feeling absolutely awful. We didn't have much money. My wife deserved a vacation more than anyone, and the money I was using for this trip could have provided it. Yet, she was at home with our kids while I was using all of our spare cash to chase some wild dream. A hobby. Child's play.

Was I delusional to think I belonged anywhere near that town? This was where the best writers in the world spend every single day building massive catalogs of great songs. I wrote on and off again as time allowed and had one or two songs that might qualify as good at best. What did I think I was going to accomplish spending our money on one quick trip to Nashville?

I realized I simply needed one person to validate this wild curiosity that had me walking the streets of music row staring at the little houses where all of the radio hits had been written and recorded for decades.

Months prior to my trip, I signed up to attend a songwriter training camp hosted by the Nashville Songwriters Association International. I entered a song I had written in their songwriting contest. It placed top ten. While I was in Nashville, I played that same song for a major music publisher. He decided not to keep it, but handed it back, looked me in the eye and said, "Keep doing what you're doing because it's working."

I got the validation I was looking for.

Something incredibly powerful had just happened. I had defined success for myself based on what was important in my life, and I had achieved my goal.

ONE LIFE, TWO PATHS

It took years for me to recognize that my journey in life was comprised of two very different paths. As I lived each day trying to find my way in the world, each path had a pull on me.

The pull of success is an external pull. Everyone can see others pursuing this external path. However, we often don't see how we ourselves are being pulled by our upbringing, circle of friends, and the world around us.

The pull of significance is an undercurrent that others can't see, and we often don't even immediately recognize it in our own lives. If we do feel it, we might provoke the fear of being different than the world around us. So, we tend to keep it to ourselves.

As the force and attraction of both success and significance grow in our lives, our instinct is to keep them separate from one another. We pursue them independently of each other.

Independent Paths

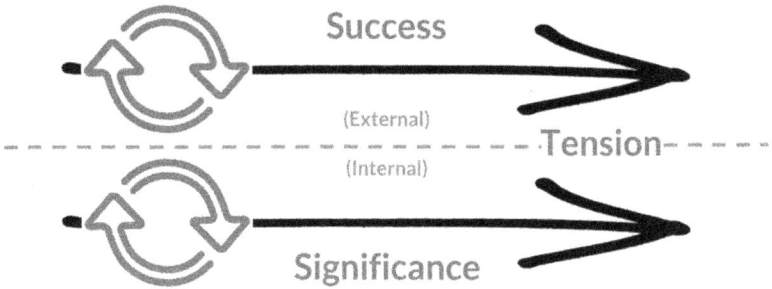

At best we allow each path to run parallel in our lives forcing us to jump back and forth between the two. At worst, we allow success and significance to run in different directions from each other. When success and significance are two completely different paths in our lives that go in opposite directions, they fight for our attention, time, and energy increasing the tension in our lives as we are forced to choose between one or the other.

Independent Paths

PUSHING BOUNDARIES

Whether we allow these paths to run parallel or pull us in opposite directions, pursuing them independently causes us to live two separate lives. This causes tension as success and significance compete for our time and energy.

The further we let these paths drift apart, the harder each pulls to get us back on their respective side. This is when we have to really be careful. The fight between these two forces in our life can cause us to be irrational at times. We can find ourselves pushing boundaries and moving from one extreme to the other.

TO THE EXTREME

If we are not careful, our pursuit of success and/or significance can become so extreme that they stop having a positive impact on us as well as others. When we take either to the extreme, our ability to add value on each path can turn to doing damage to ourselves and others.

Danger Zone

For example, were someone to put the pursuit of success above all else, they might feel no qualms about participating in a Ponzi scheme. Rather than giving and contributing who they are to find success, they actually go against who they are by taking from others. They damage their reputation and risk severe consequences.

Were someone to pursue significance above all else, they might choose to support a cause they don't even believe in. Rather than doing what they love, they can get caught using the pursuit of a cause that others would view as significant in an effort to advance their external goals of recognition rather than to feed their personal calling. In this instance, they are left with no personal sense of significance when they engage in the right things for the wrong reasons.

CREATIVE SIDE OUT HANDBOOK

1. Success and significance compete for our time, energy, and attention before we are even aware that they are at work in our lives.

2. When we treat success and significance as two independent paths, it creates tension in our lives. This tension stems from the world's external definition of success competing with our internal desire for meaning and importance.

3. As we are influenced to fight our way back and forth between success and significance, we have to be careful to not take either too far to the extreme where we might actually do damage to ourselves and others.

DISCOVER & EXPLORE YOUR PATH

1. Reflect on what competes for your time, energy, and attention and write each down. Now label each of them as "success" or "significance" depending on what the driving force is behind them. Is the pull of each goal oriented and driven by the external world of success? Or do they have meaning and importance and are driven by the internal desire for significance?

2. Compare the two groups of responsibilities and interests you identified in the previous question. Would you

say the paths of success and significance are intertwined
and create alignment in your life or are they leading in
opposite directions causing tension?

3. How would your life be different, if at all, if you were to
forego significance in favor of success? How would your
life be different, if at all, if you were to forego success in
favor of significance?

MORE TO THE STORY

I made five or six more trips to Nashville, each leading to new
relationships, more knowledge about the business, and all while learning how to write better songs. I was ever so slightly but consistently
cracking open doors. At the same time, I was still trying to advance
my real estate career and maximize my ability to support my family.

The back and forth battle between success and significance last-
ed nearly eight years before the war completely took its toll on me.
The reality set in. Neither real estate nor songwriting was producing
the desired outcome.

The war between success and significance had exhausted me. I
knew something had to give, but wasn't sure what to do next. I ended
up retreating from both worlds. I got out of real estate completely
and I stopped writing and going to Nashville.

CHAPTER 5
CASUALTIES OF WAR

Most people don't lead their life;
they accept their life.

—John C. Maxwell

Nashville sets an extremely high bar for songwriters. The most talented musicians and writers write twice a day and crank out good songs like a machine. I wrote a song a month if I was on a roll. Their odds of hitting on a great song were way better than mine.

In Nashville, there's a sentiment that you must be present to win. I already knew I wasn't going to uproot my family and move to Nashville. My wife and I loved where we lived. It was the perfect place to raise our boys. Our schools were top notch. The church we loved was right down the street. Our parents weren't too far away.

I was willing to make sacrifices for myself, but I was not willing to force my family to sacrifice their quality of life on my behalf. At the same time, I realized that the odds of me finding success in Nashville from Texas were worse than winning the lottery.

In Texas, I had entered the field of real estate development to make as much money as possible, but the truth was that all of my friends made more money than me. I was a worker bee making a set salary. I now had a growing family and my company didn't even have health insurance or a 401k. On top of that, the mortgage industry had just been dealt a massive blow and the real estate market was crashing.

Faced with these dismal prospects, I left my job and entered a management training program for a world-class company in a completely different industry. Training started at the bottom. I went from being the Vice President of Real Estate Development working on multi-million dollar deals to a non-titled employee checking stock and pulling orders in a warehouse.

As I rotated through different positions in the program over the next few years, my only responsibility was to learn the role of each position. I didn't have to make critical decisions and performance of the company was not on me. I simply showed up, did my job, and went home. It was a welcome change and much needed break from the war I had been fighting since graduating grad school. During this time, I didn't worry about success and money, and I didn't make any trips to Nashville. In fact, I didn't write at all.

The time away from both worlds gave me the opportunity to decompress, step back, and evaluate the path I had been on and where I was going in life. Removed from the heat of the battle, I could see the extreme swings I had made jumping back and forth between real estate and songwriting.

I had tried to satisfy the call for both success and significance. Pursing each separately wore me down so that at times I had no fight left in me. The war took its toll, and no matter which side I chose, I would be forced to settle for less than everything I wanted in life.

I had spent enough time in the extremes that the far ends of both sides illuminated the roles that success and significance truly played in my life. I was beginning to understand the effects of each on my life and, more importantly, the effects that the absence of each had when I abandoned them.

SETTLING FOR SUCCESS

Material success in and of itself isn't a bad thing. We all strive for it and need it in our lives. It plays a critical role in how we add value to our own lives and the lives of those around us.

When we go all in on success and ignore or limit significance in our lives, we don't know why we are pursuing the tasks, milestones, and goals we reach for. When we become materially successful we reap external rewards but are left with a feeling that something's missing.

Something's Missing

Success

(External)

Is something missing in life?

When we choose the extreme of success our goals are not rooted in meaning and importance. Achieving them doesn't carry much fulfillment and satisfaction.

SETTLING FOR SIGNIFICANCE

Significance is what we all truly desire. We want to know that what we do and who we are has meaning and importance in this world. Significance is rooted in process and is connected to how we use our unique natural curiosity, interest, and abilities. It is our adult form of play.

We discover a natural passion and are drawn to it. We explore it. We embrace it. We use it and we grow it. What starts as an interest becomes a part of our identity. When we engage in it, the process of pursuing that interest is fulfilling and satisfying. We know that it has meaning and importance and could potentially positively impact others, but we fear what others will think, and keeping it to ourselves keeps us in our comfort zone.

Something More

Is there something more to life?

When we keep our personal source of significance to ourselves, we don't give it room to fully blossom. Our natural curiosities and abilities never get the chance to inspire and encourage the world around us. We don't make the impact we want to make in the world, and we are left feeling that there must be something more to our lives.

CREATIVE SIDE OUT HANDBOOK

1. If we force ourselves to choose between a life of success and a life of significance, we settle for less than the life we deserve and are called to live.

2. When we go with the flow of life and try to achieve success as defined by the world around us, we can be left with a void or that *something's missing* feeling despite our accomplishments.

3. When we keep our source of significance to ourselves, we strangle it and don't give it room to impact and inspire the world around us.

DISCOVER & EXPLORE YOUR PATH

1. When you step back, slow down, and evaluate, do you see anywhere along the way where you decided "good enough" was good enough? Were there any times where you stopped short of your destination and settled?

2. Can you identify the milestones and goals you have achieved that did not bring the satisfaction, fulfillment, and happiness that you expected? Have you ever achieved a goal only to be left with that 'something's missing' or 'there's got to be something more to life' feeling?

3. Is there anything in your life that you pursue alone or in private that provides meaning and importance to your life? If you shared that part of your life with others could it potentially inspire them and impact them in a positive way?

MORE TO THE STORY

When I decided to leave real estate, I truly believed that I could be happy in a different industry. I had found a world-class organization with top-notch leadership. The company knew exactly what their brand was, what their core business was, and knew how to train people for massive success in their system.

I was wrong. I loved the company, but hated the industry. I couldn't force myself to read and learn about it. While ninety percent of the people that went through the training went on to find huge success with the company, I knew I wouldn't be one of them. My heart was not in it, and I was taking up a position that someone else would thrive in.

Real estate was recovering from the most recent crash. I had spent three years out of real estate and done very little in terms of music and writing. I knew it was time to make my way back to both real estate and writing, but I also knew I couldn't go back to the extreme swings back and forth between the two.

If I was going to return to both, I needed to have a different mindset. I needed to know exactly what role each played in my life. I needed to know why I wanted to return to real estate and writing.

CHAPTER 6
FINDING OUR PEACE

Clarify your purpose. What is the why behind
everything you do? When we know this in life
or design it is very empowering
and the path is clear.

—Jack Canfield

I had spent enough time away from both real estate and writing that the wounds from the war between success and significance were healed. I felt the urge to return to both, but I knew I had to have a better plan this time. I needed to know why I was compelled to return to both and to clearly define my expectations for what I needed from each path in my life. I needed to ensure I could find peace in returning to both paths so that the war did not ensue again.

I put both real estate and writing through the why drill. I asked myself why I wanted to write. Then in response to my answer, I asked myself why again. I repeated that sequence until I had asked myself why five times and had provided five answers. Then I repeated the drill again, this time asking myself why I wanted to be in real estate.

I thought I knew why I was attracted to both real estate and writing. On the surface, my answers were the same to both-to make money. However, I had never drilled down deep into why I was pursuing either path. Asking why five times forced me to go much deeper than I ever had, and the final answers for both real estate and writing were eye opening.

THE SONGWRITING "WHY" DRILL

1. Why do I want to write songs?

Answer: To get my songs recorded by major label artists.

2. Why do I want major label artists to record my songs?

Answer: To make enough money to quit my job.

3. Why do I want to make enough money to quit my job?

Answer: To spend more time in Nashville and write songs full-time.

4. Why do I want to spend more time in Nashville and write songs full-time?

Answer: To learn from the best and write with others that share this passion so that I can become the best songwriter that I can be.

5. Why do I want to be the best songwriter that I can be?

Answer: So my songs will connect with others and positively impact their lives.

That final answer was a pivotal one. It was a light bulb moment. I realized why my natural interest, curiosity, and draw toward writing never went away. Songwriting was never about becoming a professional or making money. If it had been, then it wouldn't have kept calling me.

Now it was clear why avoiding the call to use, grow, and share my writing on a regular basis had been causing tension throughout the years. Songwriting wasn't a hobby. It was purpose.

THE REAL ESTATE "WHY" DRILL

1. Why do I want to be in real estate?

Answer: To make a lot of money.

2. Why do I want to make a lot of money?

Answer: To find financial freedom.

3. Why do I want to find financial freedom?

Answer: To allow me to pursue writing full-time.

4. Why do I want to pursue writing full-time?

Answer: Writing is what I wake up and want to do every day.

5. Why do I want to write every day?

Answer: Writing satisfies and fulfills me.

That final answer was mind-blowing. That couldn't be right. I didn't get into real estate because something outside of real estate satisfied and fulfilled me. I got into real estate to be successful. I remember graduating high school and going to college because I wanted to be successful like all of my private school friends' parents. I wanted to make a lot of money, have a nice big house, new cars, a corner office, take vacations around the world, and play golf at the country club as a member.

Getting to the root of why I wanted to pursue real estate revealed so many eye-opening truths in my life. I didn't care about money and things as much as I thought I did. Success wasn't really about material things to me. It was about doing what I loved on a daily basis to provide satisfaction and fulfillment in my life. I was only in real estate, or any other day job for that matter, so that I could write.

I now completely understood the war that had erupted between success and significance in my life. The cause of the war could be traced back to my definition of success (or actually, my lack of a definition). To make matters worse, I had been applying the world's definition of success not only to my real estate career, but also to my writing, resulting in neither path providing me what I needed.

To add to the tension, I had always made real estate the default priority and treated writing like a hobby. I had used writing as an outlet from my day-to-day real estate world. I had it backwards. I was a writer first and foremost. Writing should have always been my core focus, and real estate was something I did to support my writing.

Discovering my why provided me with the clarity needed to find peace. I was now aware of the roles success and significance played in my life, and I recognized my natural interest and curiosity in writing as a call to be myself. In order to find peace, I needed to create the space to give writing the time and attention I now knew it required in my life.

JOINING FORCES

When success and significance are kept on separate paths in our lives, they compete for our time, energy, and attention. They pull us apart, stretch us thin, and ultimately limit the impact we have on this world.

Combined Paths

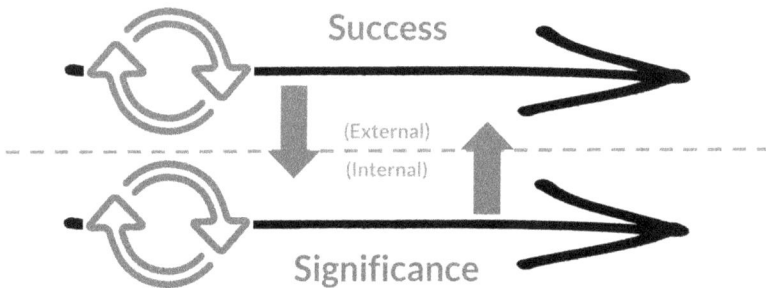

However, when we start to merge the two paths into one and let them work together, we multiply our ability to add value to our lives and the lives of those around us.

When we use success and significance in our lives in conjunction with one another, they will feed each other to close the gap in our lives.

LIFE TO THE FULLEST

When we allow significance to guide our path to success, it fosters an environment that allows us to fully live the life we were meant to live to the fullest of our abilities.

We have to use our natural internal interests and curiosities to define our external tasks, milestones, and goals. When we allow significance to determine and define our success, we draw out our internal meaning and importance into the world.

Combined Paths

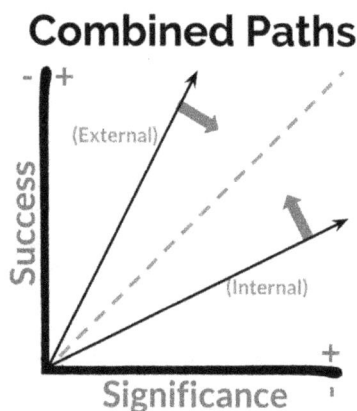

MAXIMIZING OUR IMPACT

When we put our natural inner curiosities and interests into the external world for others to benefit from, we give others the opportunity to find meaning and importance from our work.

As we allow these two realms of our existence to draw one another in and strengthen each other, we get better at what we do. We add more and more value to the world, and we start having an impact that people notice.

They will tell others about what we are doing and the impact we are having on them. They will even begin trading their dollars for the value we provide allowing us to support our families and continue doing what we love.

CREATIVE SIDE OUT HANDBOOK

1. Before we can find peace between success and significance, we have to know why we want to pursue each path and clarify the role we need each to play in our lives.

2. When we discover our why, we discover who we truly are and can then use what satisfies and fulfills us to redefine our own authentic definition of success.

3. Once we embrace our natural interest and curiosity, know why we are attracted to it, and define success for ourselves, we can then draw on our drive to succeed, defined and supported by our desire for significance to live the life we were called to live, and maximize our impact on the world.

DISCOVER & EXPLORE YOUR PATH

1. What are the surface-level "whys" for the things you are currently pursuing or want to pursue in your life? Do the why drill for each of the above pursuits. After completing the "why" drill, label which pursuits feel more like a hobby or side interest and which have surfaced as a potential call in your life. Based on your "why" drill answers, can you draw any conclusions to the roles that you need success and significance to play in your life?

2. Now take some time to redefine success in your own words on your own terms of what is important and has meaning in your life. Make sure your personal definition of success reflects your true self based on what satisfies and fulfills you.

3. How could you let these different paths you've been pursuing in life feed one another and lead you to one centralized, focused path (the life you're meant to live)?

MORE TO THE STORY

I had discovered that peace had to begin with my internal significant path. My writing had to define and guide my external definition and path to success. Significance and success were meant to work together in harmony as opposed to against one another.

After digging deep into my why, I found clarity. Both success and significance pointed me toward writing. It was time to make changes in my life to allow both success and significance to work together in harmony. Symbols of that peace began to surface and keep me motivated to live the life I was being called to live.

CHAPTER 7

SYMBOLS OF PEACE

Happiness is when what you think, what you say,
and what you do are in harmony.

—Mahatma Gandhi

Discovering that writing was more than a hobby for me, was a pivotal moment in my life. I finally realized it was a part of my identity that I was supposed to embrace. That discovery brought peace to my soul. The path I was supposed to walk in life came into focus. I knew that I had to take my inner call to write and put it into action in the external world.

I had a cheap wristband made to remind me to not let a day slip by without pursuing my calling and sharing it with the world. I created a simple logo for the wristband that read "Creative Side Out." That wrist band became a symbol of peace for me. Motivated and inspired with it on, I made some strategic changes to my environment and daily routine to help me start moving down the path I knew I was being called to walk in life.

For years we had a home office in our house. It looked like a traditional home office. I had a large desk in the middle of the room with a lamp and two computer monitors on it. I had a massive bookcase full of real estate text books, a ton of hardcover fiction novels, pictures of family, and a few strategically placed awards. I had a few guitars hanging on a wall, but there was no doubt this was an office and not a studio.

With my newfound understanding of the role writing played in my life, it was time to change all that. I removed everything from the room and repainted it. I made and bought new furniture, hung every instrument I owned on the walls, put acoustic treatment up, permanently set up all of my recording equipment, and turned that room into a studio. I physically, mentally, and emotionally made writing the focus of my world. Now there is no doubt; whoever walks by that room recognizes it is a creative environment.

After transforming my home office into a studio, I created a small window of time to engage in writing every day. I found thirty minutes in the morning before work. I aimed to write one song a week. Soon, I noticed it was working. They were not all good songs, but I was finishing them.

I realized how good it felt to do what I wanted to do every day before anything else got in my way. It began to change my tone and attitude in life. I was happier. I found satisfaction and fulfillment first thing in the morning. This made me more present at work during the day and more present at home during the evening.

Answering the call to write was only part of the change of focus in my life. The longer my writing streak, the more songs I wrote. The more songs I wrote, the more I began to believe in myself and could confidently tell people I was a songwriter.

In the past, a handful of key people close to me knew that I wrote, but I was not likely to tell those I wasn't close to about my writing. That began to change. I told people that I hardly knew. And I wasn't just telling them that I wrote in my spare time. I told them that I was a writer and working toward one day doing it full-time.

In the past, I never played my songs much for my wife. As I began to write three or four songs a month, I wanted to know which ones she liked best and why. The feedback helped me write better songs the next month. My songs were beginning to connect with her.

I realized that we had added a mutually beneficial element to our relationship centered around my songs. I wanted to play them and get feedback. She wanted to hear them and connect to the emotion behind them. Together, we formed a cycle of positive connection.

While I was still not creating income from doing what I loved, I was actively working to close the gap between success and significance in my life. I was learning to be myself by embracing, producing, and sharing my songs and revealing to others what my passion was. I was working toward merging the paths of success and significance so that they could become one combined path working in unison. I was beginning to live Creative Side Out.

THE LIFE WE ARE MEANT TO LIVE

Living Creative Side Out means living the life we were meant to live. We embrace who we are and the call to our natural interests and curiosities. We use and grow those interests and abilities. Then, when we share who we are and what we love doing, we begin to positively impact others, which in turn begins to positively impact our own lives.

Our desire to find significance, meaning and importance in our lives defines the tasks, milestones, and goals we set for ourselves. In other words, we not only begin to define success for ourselves, but we then proceed to check those boxes, cross those milestones, and achieve goals that provide us a sense of satisfaction and fulfillment.

When our definition of success is rooted in what has meaning and importance to us, we are able to live one life on one single path with all of our being. We embrace who we are, do what we love, and share what we do. We live Creative Side Out.

Creative Side Out

Creative Side Out

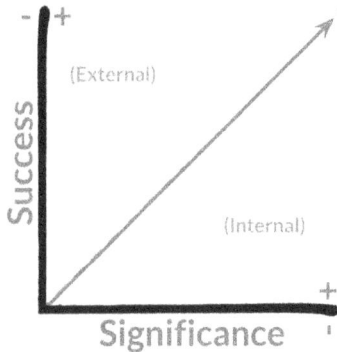

LIVING CREATIVE SIDE OUT

Merging the path of success and significance is a powerful movement in our lives, but it is not easy. In order to get there, we must face our fears and get out of our comfort zone.

Living Creative Side Out requires that we risk being judged. We may be seen initially as different and not blending in with the crowd or our circle of influence. We have to continually fight the fear and discomfort that works against us and tries to bribe us to turn around and go back to what everyone else is doing. We have to decide that we don't care what others will think, embrace our own identity, and give it space in the external world to grow.

We have to break down everything we know and have been taught about success so that we can reengineer our definition of success to one that is personal, rooted in meaning and importance, and unique to our life.

To live Creative Side Out means to live the life we were meant to live instead of the life that the rest of the world expects us to live. We embrace who we are and what we are called to do. We use and grow that natural, consistent call that won't back down. We commit to it and give it space in the external world to grow and work its magic in our lives and those of others.

CREATIVE SIDE OUT HANDBOOK

1. When we allow success and significance to draw closer to each other and work together in our lives, we begin to display our inner creativity in the outside world and live Creative Side Out.

2. Living Creative Side Out allows who we are to identify the tasks and milestones necessary to achieve our goals and have success while still finding satisfaction and ful-

fillment in doing what we love.

3. We begin transitioning our lives to living Creative Side Out by changing our mindset, controlling our lifestyle, and repositioning ourselves to maximize our impact on ourselves as well as the world around us.

DISCOVER & EXPLORE YOUR PATH

1. Which path from the previous chapter questions do you feel drawn the strongest toward pursuing? What is your most important goal that if achieved would provide you success rooted in significance? How can success and significance work together to help you focus on your one true path in life and pursue your most important goal?

2. Taking the dominant path and goal you selected from the previous question, what milestones need to be crossed to get you from your current reality to that goal? Once you've identified those milestones, fill in the tasks required to get you from one milestone to the next.

3. What changes can you create in your daily environment to physically and emotionally help spend more time focused on pursuing the goal that is your one true path in life? These could be daily reminders, symbols, or changes to your physical environment or daily routine. I would also encourage you to create a phrase, initials, or even logo as a personal brand that represents who you are and what you are being called to pursue in life. Print it, draw

it, or have it on a wearable so that you see it every day to remind you to pursue your journey and motivate you.

MORE TO THE STORY

As I began to drive the path of success and the path of significance closer to each other, I began to fully understand that they had to become one, consolidated path. I knew I had to not only continue on the path I had found, but I needed to find more time every day to live Creative Side Out.

In addition to my wristband, I had a hat made with my Creative Side Out logo on it. I set the logo as my desktop wallpaper on my computer. I had stickers printed that I strategically placed. My wife even had custom logo coasters made for me that I put in my studio.

Like my wrist band and home-office-turned-studio, the hat, stickers, and coasters all became symbols of peace in my life. The logo and those three simple words were a daily reminder of where I had been and where I was determined to go in life. I had no idea that these symbols of peace and my new direction and focus in life were forming the foundation of a full blown philosophy on how to live life to the fullest.

CHAPTER 8
FIVE PRINCIPLES

The key to realizing a dream is to focus not on
success but significance, and then even the small
steps and little victories along your path will take
on greater meaning.

—Oprah Winfrey

Motivated and inspired by my symbols of peace, I engaged in writing every day. I worked no matter how small the task or how little time I had to spend. I made sure to engage in the process.

I continued to share what I produced each week with my wife.

I played at more neighborhood pool parties. When we reunited with old friends, I made sure to play a song or two for them. I found an online community of like-minded songwriters. I took classes taught by professional writers. I attended writing retreats with professional writers. I regularly submitted songs to an online forum for both professional and peer feedback.

A home studio, cheap wristband, and a logo with three simple words reminded me to engage every day. Before I knew it, streaks of consistency were turning into habits. Habits were becoming a way of life, and my way of life was drawing my true internal self into the external world for all to see.

Before this new commitment, I'd come home too tired to engage in my writing and then I'd be upset that another day was going to slip by without answering the call. But now my mornings were filled with satisfaction and fulfillment from showing up and answering the call to write. This allowed me to be more present at work during the day. It also provided for a guilt-free evening.

Guilt-free evenings and weekends helped me to be more present for my family. Because I had more energy in the evenings, I could also spend free time engaged in learning. I watched videos, read books, took online classes, and listened to podcasts in order to obtain tips and tricks that I could apply to my process. However, I wasn't just trying to grow my songwriting. I was watching and reading about self-improvement, productivity, entrepreneurship, art, and commerce. I was discovering new authors and teachers as well as reconnecting with those I had encountered earlier on my journey.

The constant mix of doing, sharing, and learning unveiled powerful insights to me. As I reread the concepts in books like *The Artist's*

Way by Julia Cameron and multiple titles by Matthew Kelly, their teachings made more sense and rang truer in my life than they had the first time I read them.

Everything I was discovering and experiencing on my journey was touched upon in books I had read many years ago. However, after living through my own struggles, I better understood the teachings of those authors.

I began to mix and match concepts from different authors and speakers. I modified and expanded them to apply specifically to my experiences. As I combined the teachings passed on by others with my personal journey to write, five guiding principles emerged that summarized the truths I had discovered.

Five Principles

| All Seek Significance | Everyone's Creative | Product & Process | Creative Cycle | Higher Power |

WE ALL SEEK SIGNIFICANCE

The Creative Side Out way of life stemmed from the revelation of one powerful guiding principle. Despite striving for success, significance is what we all truly seek. When we make the decision to embrace, use, grow, and share our natural interest and curiosity, we develop a mindset that creates the conditions necessary for success and significance to work together in our lives. We make the decision to put who we are and what we love to do ahead of all external signs of success.

EVERYONE IS CREATIVE

Creativity is not reserved for only those that engage in the arts. Creativity comes in many forms that aren't always obvious. We all have it, even if we think we don't. Creativity is simply applying one's original curiosity and thought to modify existing ideas and products to form something new and valuable. Creativity happens in every discipline from science to education to philosophy, technology, theology, business, and so forth.

Sure, artists create paintings and sculptures. Comedians write and tell jokes. Musicians create melodies and harmonies combined with lyrics. Actors and actresses bring characters to life in a believable way that we can relate to. Woodworking craftsmen build furniture. However, there are many ways that inner creativity surfaces and makes an impact through others that we wouldn't consider to be in the arts or call a craftsman.

Human resource managers develop creative approaches to matching the right candidate to the right position that will also complement the other team members. Social workers find new ways to connect with and counsel others. Consultants live for and thrive on finding new ways to grow efficiency. Marketers break the mold and make new waves for their clients' products and services. Pet trainers look for new ways to teach humans how to interact and understand their animals. Farmers are constantly creating innovative ways to cultivate their land and incorporate new and exciting practices on their homestead.

We all have something that we are drawn to that occupies our time and attention. That natural draw is our own north star, guiding us to our inner creativity, and we all have it.

PRODUCT AND PROCESS

When we embrace our inner creativity, we engage in our own unique process, which in turn results in a product. Both product and process play critical roles in shaping our happiness in life.

Engaging in process satisfies our call and natural curiosity. Process uses and grows that curiosity. Through the process of trial and error, we improve our craft. When we engage in process, we show up, we explore, and we allow our inner creativity space to play. Engaging in our own process on a consistent basis is our source of internal fulfillment and satisfaction.

Our product is the result of us engaging in our process. It can be a tangible product, such as a piece of furniture, a painting, or a cake. It can also be an intangible product such as a system we implement, a performance we give, or guidance we provide. Regardless of the form it takes, our product is something we can share with the external world.

THE CREATIVE CYCLE

Engaging in process and sharing our product creates a cycle that helps us gain momentum, increase our influence, achieve success, and find significance. The Creative Cycle is one of humanity's most beautiful natural systems. We get to be ourselves and do what we love. Others get to benefit from what we do. Others will encourage us emotionally and support us financially when we add value to their lives which allows us to keep doing and growing what we love and are called to do.

HIGHER POWER

When we feel a natural call to something that continues to interest us and naturally draws us toward it, we begin to discover who we truly are. As we embrace that call, our true authentic self begins to surface. When we hear a voice calling us, and we answer that call, we are embracing who we were created to be.

Through my own experiences, I have come to know that voice as God. Some will be comfortable calling that higher power God while others will be more comfortable calling it a higher power, guiding force, creative energy, or the universe. What is important is that we acknowledge that there is a higher power at work in our lives, and it is the inherent good inside of us guiding us to live the life we are being called to live.

When we use and grow our natural interest and curiosity, we add value to our lives and the lives of those around us. As we positively impact people's souls, including our own, we are living the life our higher power is calling us to live.

When we encounter others that embrace their inner creativity, we see people that have found happiness and importance in their lives. They have something intangible that makes them radiate, and we want that in our lives. We all are called to have that same radiance in our own lives. When we have faith and are true to ourselves, engage in process, and share our product and process, we are rewarded with true happiness.

CREATIVE SIDE OUT HANDBOOK

1. While the world around us is obsessed with the path to material success, the path of significance is the one that we all truly seek in our lives.

2. We all have an *inner creativity* or natural interest and curiosity, and the Creative Cycle is how we find satisfaction and fulfillment on a regular basis by engaging that interest and curiosity to produce something of value we can share with the world.

3. There is a higher power or guiding force directing us to find joy through our journey to discover our inner creativity, embrace it, use it, grow it, and share our product and our process with the world to live the life we were meant to live here on Earth and have a positive impact on people's souls, including our own.

DISCOVER & EXPLORE YOUR PATH

1. Reflect on a time when you engaged in your own creative process. What is your own personal Creative Cycle? What does it feel like to be in the flow? Now contrast the previous answers with a time when you were engaged in something solely for material success. What was the difference?

2. What does creativity mean to you? What subjects attract your natural interest and curiosity so that you begin to try and modify existing techniques to find your own unique process and develop your own unique product? Who could benefit from you showing them your own unique process or product? What potential benefits do your product and process offer others? With whom could you share your process and product with?

3. Reflect on the role of your own higher power in your personal creative process. Do you feel like when you are engaged in your natural interest and curiosity that you are drawing from a higher power? Do you feel like you are serving a higher power?

MORE TO THE STORY

As these five principles emerged through my experiences and the teachings of others, the words "Creative Side Out" began to represent more than just writing and sharing my songs. Those three words began to represent everything I wanted from life.

I found myself compelled to start documenting my journey and the lessons I'd learned in a way that could be passed on to my kids and that they could pass on to their kids. It didn't take long for me to realize that my call to create wasn't only to write songs. I was being called to write this book.

In a way, I was right back where I started. I was torn between career and call. The difference was that I knew the function of each in my life. While I was obligated to do my best work to help my company be successful, it was not my calling. It was a means to support my family. Real estate was a contract. I would do good work. They would pay me good money. Writing, whether it be as a songwriter or an author, was how God intended for my existence and journey to have a maximum lasting impact on this world.

I needed to give this book the time, energy, and attention it deserved on a regular basis. I needed to teach my kids that transitioning our lives to fully living Creative Side Out starts with productivity. That's how I began my journey as a songwriter. I simply needed to do the same for my book writing.

CHAPTER 9
DO WHAT YOU LOVE

What we really want to do is what we are really meant to do. When we do what we are meant to do, money comes to us, doors open for us, we feel useful, and the work we do feels like play to us.

—Julia Cameron

I loved the idea of being a commercial songwriter, so much so that I had attended workshops in Nashville to learn techniques from the best songwriters in the world. I had paid for demos by professional musicians, vocalists, and producers. I had pitched those demos to industry decision makers and even gotten encouraging feedback that had inspired me to keep working at it.

Over the last decade, I had taken a good amount of action. However, I never really built any lasting momentum because I had been treating my writing like a hobby. I worked on writing when I was inspired to do so, and I would drop it the second I got busy, tired, or distracted. Without momentum, I would fall out of the groove and my pursuit would dwindle.

At this point in my journey, I had discovered the role of success and significance in my life. I knew I wanted those two to work in unison. What I didn't know was how to transition my life in a direction that would allow that to happen.

I knew I had to change my mindset and start thinking of myself as a writer in the same way I thought of myself as a real estate professional. I needed to be able to confidently say and believe the words "I'm a writer." Just like anything else, those words felt awkward at first. I wasn't sure I believed them myself.

I thought about why I was comfortable calling myself a real estate professional and not a writer. The difference was not a paycheck and benefits. It was that I showed up to engage in my real estate work every day. I showed up much less frequently to write. I had been dedicated to real estate and treated writing like a hobby.

I had to make writing a priority that was given the same amount of time or more than other areas of my life. I made a conscious decision to become more consistent, which meant developing new habits designed to be more productive and build that much-needed momentum. I also knew to keep showing up and doing the work consistently, I needed to WANT to keep showing up. For me, that meant I needed little victories to keep pushing me forward.

I was already an early riser and loved spending the mornings outside in the quiet darkness before the sunrise. I reallocated some of that time and began writing twenty-five minutes each day. Twenty-five minutes turned into forty-five minutes. Then an hour. Before I knew it, I was spending two hours each day in the early mornings writing. My first little victory was matching my productive sessions with a time of the day and place that I already enjoyed.

My second little victory was to set manageable expectations of how to use that time each day. When I first started utilizing the mornings like this, I wanted to write a song every week. I would start by knowing what idea or title I wanted to write Sunday night. I used the first few days of the week to write the chorus. The rest of the week was reserved for verses and a bridge if necessary. That goal still seemed a little daunting given that I previously wrote one song every month or two.

So, I set the expectation for myself even lower. I considered my daily writing successful if I was able to produce two good lines in those two hours. That was it. That was not hard, and usually two good lines would inspire at least two more. Before I knew it, I was producing four to eight lines easily in each session.

I started to write a song a week on a regular basis. I proved to myself that I could do it. I just had to identify the time, set the appointment, and keep showing up with the goal of writing two lines a day. That's it. As I began to trust and have faith in my process, it let me down less and less.

Little victory number three came in the form of allowing myself to suck. I put quantity over quality, recognizing that this was practice. As long as I finished my song for that week, I was content. I didn't pressure myself to write a hit. I did pressure myself to produce. I still had to show up and write words until I at least had my two lines.

After showing up on a daily basis, engaging, and finishing songs (even if they sucked), it didn't take long for me to get comfortable, gain confidence, and begin to identify myself without question as a writer. Little victories made me WANT to keep showing up and be productive. Living Creative Side Out started with productivity.

Productivity

Do What You Love

Productivity is like water that permeates down below the surface and nurtures the seed, roots, and core of our being. Productivity grows us on the inside. It provides nutrients to our soul.

As long as we keep engaging, tinkering, and improving our process, what looks and feels like play begins to turn our natural interest and curiosity into a skill.

The process of engagement eases the tension in our lives that we get from ignoring and not answering our call toward using and growing our natural interests.

Productivity becomes our default and shelter from the world around us. It is where we turn to find relief from chaos, complications, and stress of the everyday world. It is the answer to our critics and negative feedback toward our product and any attacks on who we are and what we love to do. It is also our way of stretching ourselves after our best work.

Even though we are physically and mentally engaged, productivity is a form of rejuvenation. It energizes us, drives us forward, and serves as a source of calm and peace in our lives. The process of engagement feeds our internal desire for significance by providing fulfillment and satisfaction from being ourselves.

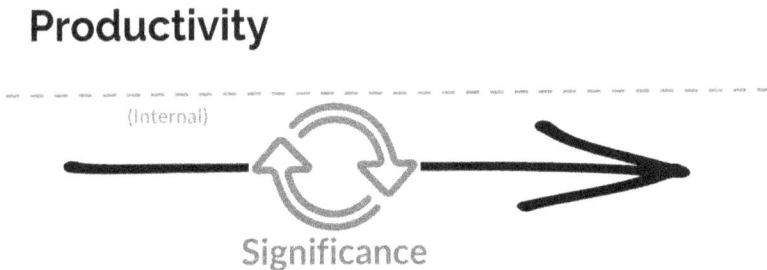

Productivity

(Internal)

Significance

Productivity is the process of transforming our natural interest and curiosity into something of value. Regular productivity is how we complete tasks, push past milestones, and achieve our external goals. When our goals are guided by our authentic interest and curiosity, we achieve a success that is rooted in significance.

DISCOVERY

Our authentic natural interest and curiosity will find a way to get our attention. When we allow ourselves to engage and explore that interest and curiosity, we are in discovery mode.

We try something new and then try it again. Chances are that we are not good at engaging in the process. We are slow, clumsy, and inefficient, but we are fascinated by this new thing. We continue to get drawn to it. We can't wait to try it again. So, we keep finding a way to engage.

That is the beginning of our authentic self, calling us to engage and grow our natural interest and curiosity. We discover our desire to get better at this activity even if it appears we have no skill or ability.

We watch others that are better than us and study them and their process. We borrow their techniques and, through a series of trial and error, adapt and utilize what works for us. We discard what doesn't.

The more we give this natural interest and curiosity time and attention, the more we engage in it and try new things. We start engaging on a regular basis. Through trial and error, we borrow techniques and improve our process.

Eventually, what started as discovery becomes a habit that we use and grow. That new thing that we tried and weren't very good at starts to show promise in our lives as something we do well. Our productive habit and unique process begin to transform our interest and curiosity into value. We recognize it, embrace it, and become

CREATIVE SIDE OUT 81

passionate about improving our process because it starts to bring satisfaction and fulfillment into our daily lives.

IMPLEMENTING PRODUCTIVITY

Productivity requires deliberate space in our lives. In creating that space to grow our natural interest and curiosity, we have to consider when we are going to engage, where and how we are going to engage, and what we are going to focus on.

We often convince ourselves that we need a ton of time to engage and make real progress, but we don't. For example, I utilized one hour intervals to dictate a chapter or two of this book each morning. From an outline of key points, I dictated the 50,000 word first draft in ten days.

My best time is early in the morning. The work day combined with family involvement in the evenings leaves me with no energy at night. My best opportunity to engage is immediately after waking up when I am fresh. On the rare occasions that I don't get up early and do what I love, I feel off balance. If I stay up too late the night before, I know I am putting my early morning productivity at risk. I protect that time by going to bed early.

Mornings won't work for everyone. Schedules, family, work, and other commitments will be different for everyone. We have to experiment with different times of the day until we find a small window that works for us. We expand that window and we protect it at all costs. That might mean going to bed early, skipping drinks after work, or sacrificing TV in the evenings.

We can further maximize our productivity by having a regular place to go that will throw our creative minds into action. When we have a creative space, just the act of going there can engage our minds.

I spend each morning outside for at least an hour. The backyard in the early morning is where most of my ideas and actual writing takes place. My home studio is where I put words to music, play guitar, and record songs. I tend to learn and absorb the most while driving and listening to audio books, podcasts, and radio interviews.

There are no right answers on where to engage in our process. We have to try different locations until we find the one that works for us. We need to try inside, outside, alone in private, and in busy public places. We can also try breaking our process into different parts and trying different parts in different places doing different things.

Playing in different productive locations can not only be fun, but can help if we get stuck in a creative rut. Changing where we engage can spark new ideas. We might find so much productive success in the new location that it becomes our permanent location to be productive. Testing a new location might allow us to return to our original location with a fresh perspective.

Part of creating a habit and routine is having a regular space where we go to play. When we find the right place to play, our creativity at times will start showing up simply by going there.

Once we know when and where we are going to be productive, we have to decide what we are going to focus on during the time we have allowed ourselves. We need to be prepared to use our time wisely which means knowing exactly what we are going to start on so that we can jump right into our process.

When writing songs, I know exactly what song I will be working on each morning. I decide the night before, and I even know which part of the song I will start with.

Some might feel that structure and preparation negatively impacts their creativity. I agree that exploration without boundaries is part of the productive process. Simply engaging and seeing where it takes us makes productivity fun and interesting. It is also critical to keep us engaged and grow our productivity. However, having a starting point can accelerate our exploration.

Having a place to jump into our process immediately and get started is half the battle when it comes to maximizing our productivity. Sometimes we will work on exactly what we have planned, and sometimes we will be amazed by the journey and where our starting point leads us.

When we consistently show up at the same time and same place every day to engage, our creativity doesn't let us down. In fact, it will exceed our expectations as we give it the proper space and attention. When we create the conditions that are right and authentic to us, our scheduled time for productivity simply serves as a jump-start for our creativity.

Additionally, creativity doesn't shut down simply because the clock says our time is up. In many cases it will do quite the opposite because we got it rolling. This is when our ideas fall out like water from a hose.

Writing a song a week in my allotted time is not hard. I can do it every time I keep my daily writing appointments with myself. That doesn't mean I write good songs every week. Most I never play again after writing them. However, the most important thing is that I am productive and engage in my process. The process is what serves me. The finished song is a byproduct. Some are better than others.

Showing up each week and keeping the appointment produces repetition and quantity. Repetition and quantity lead to growth and improvement, and more importantly, detachment. I complete the songs, step back and see what I created, push them aside, and start over. Every now and then, one turns out better than the rest and goes into a separate stack. Those are the ones I will play more, play for others, and possibly demo.

Our job is to create the conditions that make it easy for us to keep getting little victories so that we keep showing up. The more we show up and engage in process, the more we allow productivity to do its job in our lives, which is to provide us daily doses of internal satisfaction and fulfillment.

PRODUCTIVE GROWTH

Even though we are creating repeatable habits when we engage in productivity, we don't want those habits to become stagnant and predictable. We don't want them to start to bore us. If they do begin to bore us, and we can't reignite our interests, the interest we are currently pursing may not be our true authentic call.

As long as we are naturally driven to continue to learn and eager to improve our ability, our productivity will continue to be our source of fulfillment and satisfaction in our lives. It will remain our true authentic call.

We grow and improve our productivity by allowing ourselves to play without consequence. We use trial and error and rely on what works for us to guide us as to what to keep doing and what to discontinue.

We find mentors, trade notes, and borrow techniques from others. We keep, tweak, and implement what naturally works and improves our process and learn from what doesn't. What doesn't work and improve our productivity defines our unique process just as much as what does.

It is important to note that what we are called to do can change throughout our lives. When we start to lose that natural desire to learn more, perhaps we are moving into a different season of life. We may start to feel a call to do something else in life.

The only way to know is to give the new interest space to grow. If it is an authentic call, our natural interest will continue to be more and more drawn in that direction. If it is a distraction, our authentic call will bring us back to our natural interest and curiosity.

CREATIVE SIDE OUT HANDBOOK

1. Living Creative Side Out starts with productivity: creating the space and habits that make us want to show up each day to engage and transform our natural interest and curiosity into something of value that the world might benefit from.

2. The point of doing what we love on a regular basis is not the product we create, but rather the internal growth, satisfaction, and fulfillment we get from engaging in a process that is so fun it feels like play.

3. Productivity is our inner creativity in motion, our default and reset, as well as our sword and our armor that protects and preserves who we are. It is the answer to our critics, our best work, and our best option when we simply don't know what to do.

DISCOVER & EXPLORE YOUR PATH

1. List several possibilities of a time, place, and space where you could go to get into a productive flow. Now choose when and where you would like most to start.

2. Identify and list any little victories that you feel like would motivate you to engage. Make these ridiculously simple goals. Then for each little victory, list a starting point that can serve as a catalyst to get you into the

CREATIVE SIDE OUT   87

flow as quick as possible each time you engage. Don't be afraid to make this something silly and fun. Remember that it needs to be something that you look forward to and want to do. It should feel like play.

3. Remember, productivity and engagement is the answer to criticism. Develop a strategy that will get you back into engaging in your work for the next time anyone criticizes or praises your call, process, or product. How can you set productivity as your reset and default mode?

MORE TO THE STORY

For the first time in my life, I was finishing songs on a regular basis. The more songs I finished, the more I kept wanting to show up, and the easier it became to write without consequence. I knew some songs would be better than others while most would turn out to simply be practice.

I was becoming a writer, and the more I wrote, the more I started to feel the desire to share my songs and see if they would connect with others. However, even though I could sense that my writing was starting to grow and my songs were getting better, the thought of sharing them was out of my comfort zone. When I was alone, I wanted to share them. When I had an audience, fear still held me back.

CHAPTER 10
SHARE WHAT YOU DO

*Life is about creating and living experiences
that are worth sharing.*

—Steve Jobs

For years I was not generous with my songs because sharing them made me feel vulnerable. I was becoming good at being productive, but I was still scared to share my songs because I was fearful about what others might think.

The more I wrote every day, the better the songs became. My urge to share my songs became too strong to ignore. I knew I had to overcome the fear of what others would think and put my songs out into the world. I wasn't sure that the fear of what others would think would ever go away, but two things helped me begin to share and slowly helped me to share more and more.

I started by finding like-minded people on the same journey as me to share with. I found song circles online and in person. I joined groups with other writers like me with the same natural interest and draw to writing. Together we all had a passion for growing our craft, and we provided a safe, supportive, and encouraging environment to share and learn from one another.

As part of several like-minded groups, I began to let my guard down. I played my songs and began to see the impact that songs I had written could have on others. The songs themselves started to have value in the eyes of others when I shared them. People laughed at funny songs, had fun to party songs, cried at sad and emotional songs, and found inspiration from songs that conveyed a message that was exactly what they needed at that moment.

Experiencing these reactions to words and music that I had created triggered a shift in my mindset on sharing my songs. I started to feel an obligation to share them with others. My regular productivity could only add value to the world if I shared the finished songs. Finding like-minded people in a safe environment was the first thing that helped me overcome my fear of playing my songs for others. As a result of playing for others, I realized that the finished songs weren't for me. The process of writing the songs was for me. The songs themselves were for others.

The process of writing every day is what I craved. Doing the work, putting pen to paper, and strumming guitar is what resolved the tension and satisfied my need to create. Through experience and help from Julia Cameron's book, *The Artist's Way*, it finally sank in that the finished song was merely a byproduct of the process.

In fact, the more I thought about it, a finished song kept to myself was no different than any other material thing the rest of the world identified as a symbol of success. Finished songs brought a temporary happiness, just like money, a new car, a new corner office, or new whatever. As I finished each song, I was driven to reengage in the process to find happiness and fulfillment once again.

However, sharing that finished song with others changed it from a material product to something of value that was useful and a meaningful resource. Sharing the song created an interaction with others. If that interaction was one that others connected with every time I played that song, all of a sudden the product had lasting significance.

Writing and sharing became a continuous cycle that benefited others as well as myself. The reactions to my songs, good or bad, also provided me feedback. That feedback guided me to continually improve. It inspired me to throw myself right back into what I needed most-the process of writing.

The finished songs became a way for me to measure the results of my process. Each new song I shared became a new benchmark for my writing process. It helped me keep my writing process interesting. I tried new things. I shared the songs. I got results. Then I'd write more.

Sharing accelerated my growth, increased my confidence, created impact, and helped me gain momentum.

Generosity

Share What You Do

If productivity is water that permeates below the surface and nurtures the seed of our authenticity, generosity is the sunlight that draws our inner beauty into the outside world. Generosity grows us on the outside. It provides the incremental, measured improvement that drives us toward success.

If we simply produce without sharing, we are missing out on experiencing the true magic in who we are. There are people out there that need to see, hear, and touch our products and our processes. Generosity is essential to living Creative Side Out.

Children allow their imaginations to unfold without consequence. They are not self-conscious. They are unaware of any danger in sharing. Just as when we were children, when we receive joy and fulfillment from something it is natural for us to want to share that with someone else. We want to watch the smile on their face, hear their laughter, and feel that joy and fulfillment again as we share in their experiencing it.

Sharing our creations and how we did it should feel the same as when we were children sharing early artwork with our parents. If we focus only on the possibility of positively impacting others, we allow our authenticity to add value to those around us. Their positive feedback, constructive criticism, and genuine reactions to our work grow us on the outside and feed our desire for success.

Generosity

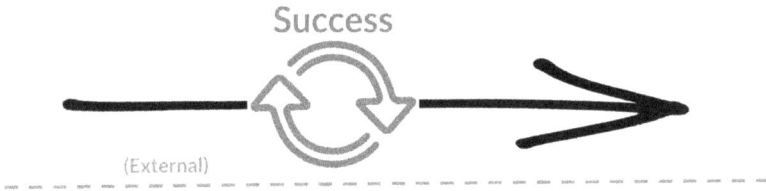

Generosity is a magical transformation of our natural interest and curiosity into value. It literally transforms what we love to do and what feels like play into something of value. The more generous we are, the better quality work we do. The better we become at using our ability and sharing it, the more value we create. Generosity allows our authentic self to put off an unmistakable radiance into this world.

OBLIGATION TO SHARE

As we discover, implement, and develop systems and techniques that improve our process, we are obligated to share them with others. We share them with those on a similar path as us, as well as with those still in search of their own authentic path.

Our process is unique. However, it is a culmination of techniques that we picked up from others that were willing to share with us. We adapt various techniques and systems. We improve our process and grow it during our existence. Our higher power calls us to not only use and grow our process, but to share what we learn with others.

All creators that document and share their process advance their craft and its impact on the world to come. We are obligated to our craft to provide a starting point for the next generation of creators to begin from.

We all start our growth from a better more advanced position than the generation of creators before us because they were willing to share their own authentic process. It's our duty to leave the next generation of creators in a better and more advanced starting position than where we started. We do this by being generous with our authentic process.

IMPLEMENTING GENEROSITY

Whether by being generous with our product or our process, there are two ways we can share what we do with the world. We can give away our process and product for free or we can charge a fee for it.

There is a balance between what we give away for free and what we charge for. We are obligated to our higher power, the world, and our craft to give some of our product and process away for free. However, we have to understand that it is perfectly acceptable to be compensated for different levels of value that we provide to others.

SHARING FOR FREE

We are all called to give away a certain amount of our process to anyone and everyone that will listen to us for absolutely free. If we have discovered our source of satisfaction and fulfillment in life, we have to expose others to our path of significance to help them find their authentic path.

Doing what we love is our source of satisfaction and fulfillment. It is also teachable. By sharing it, we can help others decide if they are called to do what we do. We can also enable those that know they are called to do what we do, but are just starting out and need some guidance.

At times, we are obligated to give our product away at no charge as well. There are people that need what we can produce with our unique process and ability. When our product has value, it can change people's lives. When we see someone in need and have the opportunity to change their life with our product, we should do so out of the kindness of our heart. That is how we make the world a better place.

We can also give away our product to gain exposure, grow our reach, and demonstrate to the world that there is value in who we are and what we do. We need an audience. We need support from fans of our product. We can introduce them to our product by giving it away.

They receive some level of value, and we gain their trust. Trust is the foundation of others' willingness to pay for our product in the future.

SHARING FOR A FEE

It's okay to charge for our product and our process. We have to pay bills, and we have to support our family. Charging a fee allows us to continue to embrace, use, grow, and share our product and process. Charging a fee is natural, and there is nothing wrong with doing so. When we provide value, we should charge a fee for it.

When we know that our product and process can genuinely have a positive impact on others and we charge for it, we trade value for value. We provide value in other people's lives in the form of our product or process, and they provide value to us in the form of financial support.

When others pay us to do what we love, it validates our authenticity. It throws us back into productivity. It encourages us to be even more generous with our product. Their payment allows us to continue to not only do what we love, but improve at it.

Charging a fee for the value we provide still makes the world a better place. In fact, it allows us to not only continue to have an impact on the world, but to increase our impact over time as we are able to spend more time being productive, improving our product, and compounding the value we create by being ourselves and doing what we love.

GENEROUS GROWTH

Just as we grow our productivity by allowing ourselves to play without consequence, we have to learn to grow our generosity by increasing our willingness to share what we do and how we do it with others.

We start sharing in small environments with others that have the similar natural interests and curiosities as we do. We share our process and push one another to improve our product in a supportive environment.

As we interact and share with others who do the same things we love to do, we begin to grow the value our authenticity adds to the world. That's when we have to move outside of our support group and begin to attract awareness from the external world to who we are and what we love to do.

As we share, we attract more fans of our work. They tell others. We begin to build momentum as we grow our comfort and ability to be generous with our product and our process and interact with others.

When we are generous with the authentic value we create, we begin to radiate and attract attention. As our audience grows, the value we provide to the world grows. We develop new relationships based on authenticity and value.

The genuine relationships that we've developed by being ourselves and doing what we love opens doors and creates additional opportunities for us to share what we do and reach our full potential.

Generosity builds momentum. It is how we maximize our impact on the world and live the life we are meant to live.

GENEROSITY IS ESSENTIAL

To fully experience the magic, power, and beauty of our authentic self, we have to take our internal source of satisfaction and fulfillment and share it with the external world.

Being transparent with our imaginative form of play is how we find purpose and significance in life. Generosity is where we allow others to benefit and find value in who we were created to be and the life we are being called to live.

Generosity is how we illuminate an unmistakable radiance into this world by simply being our genuine selves and doing what we love. People notice those that radiate. They want that in their lives. Our generosity inspires and encourages others to be authentic, productive, and generous.

Generosity is the sunlight our authentic self needs to grow who we are and what we do. It's the external world's way of shining back on us as they see the beauty in who we are. We must be generous with our product and our process to live Creative Side Out and inspire and encourage others to do the same.

CREATIVE SIDE OUT HANDBOOK

1. The more productive we are with our natural interest and curiosity, the more we will start to feel drawn to share our work with others. If we simply produce without sharing, we are missing out on experiencing the true magic in who we are.

2. Generosity is how we allow others to benefit and find value in what we love to do. It grows us on the outside, feeds our want for success, and is how we improve by letting go of our product, good or bad, and throw ourselves back into process.

3. We are obligated to give some of our product and process away for free. However, it is perfectly acceptable to be compensated for different levels of value that we provide to others.

DISCOVER & EXPLORE YOUR PATH

1. Identify a community that you could begin to share your work with on a regular basis to get feedback and learn to process that feedback both positive and negative. Where would you feel most comfortable sharing you work at first? It could be with family and friends or a specific group of like-minded creatives. Where can you learn and grow through feedback and mentoring?

2. What potential value could others receive from you sharing your product? What potential value could others receive from you sharing your process?

3. Think about what you can share with others to inspire them for free? What basic lessons, products, or product amount can you sacrifice to impact others and help them on their journey? Now, identify a place where you can reach out to consumers and offer your process and product for free. At what level will you begin to charge? Is there a milestone you can help them reach for free and then charge beyond that? How can you begin to market different packages and services at different price points that you can charge for? If you are not yet comfortable enough to think of charging for your product or your process, imagine you are and set some goals to achieve as you grow. Thinking through these ideas in the beginning and along the way helps you grow. You can always tweak and change your strategy along the way.

MORE TO THE STORY

It took me over a decade of exploring my ability to write, growing my craft, and reluctantly pushing myself to share my songs before I fully understood how my natural interest and curiosity were meant to work. Discovering how to properly use what I loved to do to positively impact others brought happiness and fulfillment to my life.

The concept was simple. When I did what I loved, it provided me with two very different things: a process and a product. I started paying more attention to the role of each and their impact on me as well as others. It was very clear that the process had the most impact on me and the product had the most impact on others.

Understanding that made it easier to share my songs. The world's feedback-good or bad-was only about how others experienced the product. It had nothing to do with me. The process was how I experienced the product. Creating the product was for me. Once it was done, it was for others.

The more I shared, the easier it became, and the more it threw me right back into productivity. What I had feared the most through the years was actually the gateway to maximizing my potential. I had to share without consequence to add value to the world. Adding value made me want to create even more. Productivity and generosity became a repeating cycle helping me gain momentum.

CHAPTER 11
REPETITION

*It's not what we do once in a while that shapes
our lives. It's what we do consistently.*

—Tony Robbins

After experimenting with the two-part Creative Cycle and realizing the impact it was having on my life, I dedicated the next year
of my life to completing the cycle as many times as possible. I relent-
lessly challenged myself to continue streaks of unbroken productivity
through process and generosity through sharing.

The more I showed up and repeated the cycle, the more I became addicted to the process and engagement. I became driven to

show up. On the days that I missed, for whatever reason, the rest of my day was off balance. I wouldn't be able to be fully present in my work and family because my universe was off kilter.

I had installed a very powerful habit in my life by showing up every day with the simple goal to write a song each week and to share it when I was done. I focused on making it around the Creative Cycle one time, producing one product, sharing it, and then repeating the cycle. I was growing and building momentum.

Every time I made it all the way around the cycle, I added one more song to my body of work. I found that with each song I added, three things happened. I started worrying less about the finished product. In other words, I began to let go of my desire to be perfect. I also found the more songs I added to my body of work, the less attached I was to them. This meant they were easier to share without consequence. Less attachment also made it easier to move on from a finished song and start the next one. Lastly, the more songs added to my body of work meant more practice both in creating and in sharing. Naturally, the more time I spent writing and sharing, the better I became at doing both.

The transition to living Creative Side Out was not going to be a quick one, but practice and repetition on a daily basis in small increments was working. I realized most songs I finished were not going to be great. I was not going to find instant success. However, I would get lucky every now and then and something great would come from one rotation through the Creative Cycle. Repetition was work, but it was work that I loved and enjoyed. I looked forward to it, and I knew if I could keep up the dedication, in several years I would be far more advanced in my craft.

In fact, after one year of staying mostly dedicated I was seeing a very noticeable difference in the quality of my writing and the reactions I was getting from listeners. My most recent songs compared to my first few songs ever written were markedly different. It was as if they were created by two different writers at two different skill levels. The first few songs were terrible and embarrassing. The more recent songs still were not to the standard of greatness found in Nashville, but they were much improved, and I was not embarrassed to play them.

I was getting better and more efficient at what I loved to do, and others were finding more value in what I was doing the more I did it. I was gaining momentum, and momentum made me want to keep doing what I loved and sharing what I was doing. I had proven to myself that the repeated cycle of producing and sharing was the clear cut path to transitioning my life and fully living Creative Side Out.

TAKE THE FIRST STEP

Repetition is work. Repetition is discipline. Repetition is how we grow, build momentum, and transform life into one of purpose. Knowing that it takes discipline and work, many of us fail to ever get started, much less finish and repeat.

Creating the right mindset, committing to change, creating space, and taking that first step might be the hardest part of creating change in our lives. Once we decide we are going to do something, we have to take the first step. We can think about what we want to do and where we want to go in life, but until we actually physically take the first step, we are only dreaming.

The first step doesn't have to be a big or difficult one. In fact, it's better if it is a small easy step. We just need a crack in the door and a tiny baby step that creates movement, no matter how incremental, in the direction we want to go.

For an aspiring author, the first step might be taking five minutes to describe the main character and what they want. For an aspiring consultant, the first step might be taking ten minutes to brainstorm a list of potential services they could offer their clients. Taking action is the difference in those that accomplish their goals and those that don't. Once we take that first step, it becomes so much easier to take one more.

CREATE A HABIT

Taking the first step creates movement. Creating a habit keeps us moving on a regular basis without hesitation. A habit is, by definition, a regular or customary practice. Furthermore, once established, it becomes hard to give up. Creating a habit forces us to take action on a regular basis. Taking action on a regular basis, no matter how small, keeps us moving forward on the path.

Like that first step, our habit should start off easy. If we try to establish a habit that takes half a day, requires a maximum amount of brain power, or requires complete isolation from the world, we are most likely setting ourselves up for failure. On the other hand, if our habit requires only ten minutes a day, doesn't require total concentration, and can be done in between tasks in our daily lives, we are much more likely to create a streak. Streaks become habits, and habits create progress.

For the aspiring writer, the habit might be as small as writing a paragraph a day showing their main character trying to get what they want. For the aspiring consultant, the habit might be calling one potential contact and informing them of the services they offer. While that author will not finish their first book in thirty days, they will have made noticeable progress over a year. That consultant will not have built a business in a month, but after twelve months should have a growing list of clients and referrals.

The great thing about a habit is that it might be difficult to start, but once established it is even harder to quit. We become addicted to our habits and, as we start to experience the slightest bit of progress through habit, we want more. With a little bit of success, that author will start writing a chapter a day and that consultant will start calling fifteen contacts a day. Creating a small habit is the doorway to instituting massive change in our lives.

PRACTICE, IMPROVE, AND GAIN CONFIDENCE

Establishing a habit makes it easy for us to show up and engage on a regular basis. It creates repetition. Repetition is practice, and practice is how we improve at anything we do. As we improve at what we do, we gain confidence. The combination of habit, improvement, and confidence is powerful. That combination creates a synergistic repetitive cycle that can positively impact our lives beyond our imagination.

Repetition

Generosity

Productivity

When we live Creative Side Out, we create the mindset and habits that facilitate improvement and confidence. We repeat the Creative Cycle over and over again. We do and share, then repeat. The more we do, share, and repeat the cycle, the more comfortable we become in who we are and what we are trying to achieve. Repetition transitions us from awkward and unsure to skilled and confident.

Writers begin to introduce themselves as writers. Consultants begin to introduce themselves as consultants. Both know where to start when they are ready to engage in their process. Both acquire and become familiar with the tools of the trade and speaking the industry jargon. Both become less nervous about sharing their work with others. Most importantly, both start to understand how to use the feedback they get from others to throw them back into process and improve their product.

CREATIVE SIDE OUT HANDBOOK

1. While taking the first step is critical to creating movement in the direction we want to go in life, continuing that movement through repetition is how we transition from awkward and unsure to skilled and confident.

2. Repetition is how we add to our body of work and become less attached to individual pieces of work, which makes it easier to share our product without consequence and quickly reengage in our process after completing our work.

3. Habits and repetition create momentum. This is the culmination of all the incremental changes we make and actions we take working together, and results in the most progress in the least amount of time to get us where we want to go in life.

DISCOVER & EXPLORE YOUR PATH

1. Rate your current reality on a scale of one to ten with one being awkward and unsure and ten being skilled and confident. Now do the same thing with where you are on achieving your goal with one meaning you are just now getting started and ten being you are consistently living how you want to live. Describe the life you want to live and what it feels like to be achieving you goals on a regular basis. Now describe you current re-

ality. What does right now look and feel like? Define a realistic goal to achieve in one year. Describe what that will look and feel like.

2. How can you build a body of work? What will your portfolio look like in terms of your interest and curiosity? How do you stay focused on building a body of work and not get sidetracked obsessing over any single piece of work?

3. Identify your Creative Cycle count goals to help you build momentum. How long does it take you to complete the Cycle one time? How many times around the Cycle is your monthly goal? How can you track your momentum? What metrics can you use to keep you motivated by your improvement and track your growth with each Creative Cycle that you complete? Set a streak goal. How many times will you regularly engage without missing in a week, month, or ninety days? What would you like to have accomplished at the end of your streak? Identify two or three specific things you would like to be more proficient at by the end of your streak and after crossing those milestones. What is the one thing that if you were more proficient at would make the biggest difference right now? Strive to cross that milestone first.

MORE TO THE STORY

With every repetition of the Creative Cycle, my transition to living Creative Side Out was happening. My quality of life was improving every day. There was a growing injection of happiness and peace in my life. I was focused on the tasks and milestones I needed to check off to achieve success as defined by me.

Life was moving in the right direction. My simple plan of repeating the cycle of productivity and generosity had proven to be a legitimate system for getting started and gaining momentum. For over a year, repeating the two-part cycle consistently provided positive movement and results in my life.

However, all of the peace, momentum, and positivity I had created in my life, was about to be stopped in its tracks. I was about to discover the hard way that in addition to productivity and generosity, there was a critical third part to living Creative Side Out.

CHAPTER 12
OPPOSITION

Beyond the fear is growth. Beyond the temporary comforts is the true comfort of knowing you are living life from your truth and not your fears.

—Athena Laz

My transition was in progress through the wonderful work-life balance I had created. The balance I had found in my life was allowing me to pursue my writing with a daily dedication that fulfilled and satisfied me. After the years of journeying, I had finally started managing success and significance in my life so that they were working in harmony. I was closing the gap between success and significance.

Then I made a decision that disrupted the balance in my life that I had worked so hard to create. I took a different real estate position with another company that demanded much more of my time, energy, and attention. My momentum came to a screeching halt. Just like that, I abandoned the path I had searched so hard to find.

I had been happy with the job I had. I loved the people I worked with. It was a great company and a peaceful and stress-free environment. Most importantly, the job I already had offered a very generous work-life balance. I was actively involved with everything my kids had going on and I had time to dedicate to my writing. Despite my journey to find the path that was right for me in life, I allowed myself to get distracted and off track.

It's not that the new company and position were a bad place to be. In fact, it was quite the opposite. It was a successful company staffed with well-respected, awesome people that had a great reputation in the industry and offered nothing but opportunity.

However, the demands and dynamics of the position I chose to take conflicted with the work-life balance I had created in my life. I was no longer working from home which meant less time with my family. My morning routines had new time constraints which severely impacted my regular writing sessions.

Set office hours, learning a new position, and interacting with more people and their needs on a daily basis also required more energy. Even when I did manage to set aside a little time to write, I found myself showing up to those sessions exhausted. I simply couldn't write on the same level as I could prior to taking the new position.

I had fought so hard over the years to find that work-life balance that allowed me to write on a regular basis to a level that satisfied me while still having an abundance of time with my family and being able to fulfill my responsibilities at work. When I made the decision to change positions, I discounted the value of that family time. I discounted the value of my writing productivity. I discounted the work-life balance.

However, I did not discount the difference in what each position paid and what each position could potentially pay over the next five to ten years. I placed a significant amount of weight on the financial aspect of the decision. I allowed fear to impact my decision. In particular, I let the fear of missing out on potential financial gains heavily influence my choice. I made a decision based on the world's definition of success and not mine.

My desire for comfort for me and my family compounded the issue. I thought if I concentrated on making money for the next decade, it would then be easier to take a risk and pursue writing. I told myself it would be much easier to jump into my creative life once we were more financially secure. So, in my head, I wasn't really abandoning the path I had worked so hard to find. I viewed taking this new position more as delaying my journey down that path while I took an excursion with potential rewards.

It didn't take me long to realize that I had underestimated the value of the work-life balance I had previously created in my life. I realized that fear and comfort were my biggest enemies when it came to living Creative Side Out and staying on the path I knew I was being called to walk. Once I was on the right path, they distracted me and threw me off track. Once again in my life, I didn't put writing first; I pushed it to the side, and treated it like a hobby.

The Opposition

ENEMIES & THEIR TRAPS

Anything worth pursuing in life will always have obstacles. Whether we know it or not, the opposition has also always been at work in our lives as we have tried to find our way. The bad news is that the opposition is never going to stay away, and no matter how good we are at battling the opposition, it will have its moments of victory. The good news is that we can win most of the battles if we know what we are up against and are prepared.

We can increase our chances of consistently defeating the opposition by knowing three things. First, we have to identify the opposition and acknowledge its presence. Second, we have to know how it works and the common traps to look out for. Lastly, we have to have a strategy and know what tactic to use to overcome the obstacle.

The opposition most frequently presents itself in one of two forms. Fear or comfort. They have always been pushing against us and always will be. As we strive to merge success and significance into the best life we can live, fear and comfort will always be there to convince us not to pursue the life we were meant to live. They will constantly try to prevent us from getting started and convince us to quit once we are in motion.

The Opposition

There are many tactics fear and comfort use in our lives to prevent us from maximizing our impact in this world. However, all of the tactics fall under two commons traps, perfection and comparison.

FEAR

When we are real, honest, and genuine with ourselves and the world, we open our hearts, our souls, and our minds and put them out there for the world to see. Living Creative Side Out, we stop making excuses for ourselves internally while at the same time, we lower our defenses to the outside world. We have to put down our guard and reveal who we truly are. That's not easy. It's tough. It's scary. Fear thrives under these conditions and is the primary opposition to living Creative Side Out.

Most of the people we encounter on a daily basis in the outside world have their guard up. That's natural. We don't want to be judged, gossiped about, or be the subject of everyone's laughter. We all want to fit in, and none of us want to get left behind. So, we put on our camouflage, blend in, and go with the flow. We protect our true identity and defend our position as we keep trying to advance in life.

We don't encounter a lot of people on a daily basis that have taken off their camouflage. We don't encounter a lot of people that reveal who they are at their very core outwardly pursing importance and meaning in their lives. It is not often that we cross paths with someone that radiates doing what they love and sharing what they do. So, we fear trying it in our own lives.

Letting down our guard to be ourselves, do what we love, and share what we do provides fear with several angles of attack and opportunities to discourage us. There is the fear of failure, the fear of missing out, the fear of getting left behind, and, the biggest of them all, the fear of what others will think of us.

FEAR OF FAILURE

Most of us want to be good at what we do, especially if others will see us engaging in the activity. For many of us, if we can't look competent at something almost immediately, we will forgo engaging at all. Fear plants the seed of doubt in us with one simple question that lingers in the back of our minds. What if we're no good at this? If we give that question the slightest bit of space to grow, fear will stop us before we even get started.

The reality is that no one is a pro at anything when starting out. We all have to start somewhere, assess our ability, chart a path to grow, and then engage and practice. Yet, we often compare our initial or early performance to someone that has engaged in the activity for a much longer period of time and is much more advanced than we are. We quickly get discouraged by comparing our early performance at something to someone that is a novice or professional.

The gap between our initial ability and that of a pro is over-whelming. How could we ever be that good? We overcome the fear of failure first by simply engaging and being productive. We continue to win when we keep showing up and making progress through rep-etition. We measure our progress against our own past performance, and we set realistic expectations to learn and grow over time. If the goal is to be a professional, we identify the milestones to get there. Then we fill the gaps between the milestones with easier, realistic, and doable tasks. Each task we perform and check off gets us closer to a milestone, facilitates growth, and builds confidence to overcome the fear of failure.

FEAR OF MISSING OUT

Throughout our lives we all face tough choices. Some are tough-er than others. In many of the life choices we have to make, saying yes to one option means closing the door to the alternatives. Choosing to attend one college, means we decline the others in consideration. Choosing a position with one company after graduation means we decline offers from others. In choosing our spouse, we eliminate the possibility of dating anyone else.

When the world around us that we live in day in and day out is moving in one direction, it is hard for us to choose a different direction. If all of our friends are going to attend one college, it makes it much harder for us to break away from the group and attend another. Even with much smaller decisions, like going out on a Friday night, it is hard for us to say no if everyone else is going. What if we don't go to the concert, all of our friends do, and it becomes the epic night they all talk about for the rest of the year?

We all experience the fear of missing out. What makes this fear even worse is that we dwell on what we could potentially miss out on. There are no guarantees that we are going to miss out on anything, but we imagine the path we could have chosen paying off to the max and base decisions on that. What if we don't go to the concert with our friends, and they get to go backstage and meet the band? What if my friends hit it off with the band so well that they all exchange numbers and become best friends?

The fear of missing out is a poisonous black hole that is hard to recover from. It causes us to play defense with our decision making. We can battle the fear of missing out by putting our decision making back on offense. Rather than concentrating on the potential what-ifs of making the wrong decision, we need to focus on the known positives of each option we could choose. We then match the known positives with our needs.

One job opportunity pays more money with bonus potential, but requires us to work sixty hours a week. Another job pays fifteen percent less with no bonus, but allows us to work from home and maximize our free time. Our minds can go into a tailspin imagining how big that bonus could be and what we could do with the extra income. We can quickly find ourselves so scared of missing out on a potential bonus that the fear controls our decision.

We take the control away from fear by eliminating the idea of the bonus from our decision making. One job is more money with less free time. One job is less money with more free time. Then we decide which best fits our needs. We then move forward confident that we have made the right decision without the fear of missing out influencing us.

Even on a lesser scale, think back to that example about going out with friends on a Friday night. Sure, we could go out and we would probably have a reasonably good time with our friends. However, we have to be honest with ourselves and recognize that the chances of it being that epic experience we are imagining in our head are slim.

Commitment to our cause promises a return on our investment of time. If we have other alternatives that we believe would better fulfill and satisfy us than going out whether it be spending time with a significant other, using that time for our own personal creative pursuits, or simply getting some much-needed rest, then we should focus on the desired outcome and what means the most to us. When we view our choices through the lens of what is important to us, we're more apt to make the right decision.

FEAR OF GETTING LEFT BEHIND

When we think of missing out in the context of the external world, our fear convinces us that those around us will not miss out.

We convince ourselves that everyone around us will always make the decisions that result in the highest payoff. Scared of getting left behind, we can find ourselves making decisions once again from a place of fear rather than from a place of sound evaluation.

None of us like the idea of getting left behind, but again we have to put our decision making on offense rather than make defensive decisions. When it comes to beating the fear of getting left behind, we do that by making sure that we are using our own authentic definition of success rather than the definition that the external world around us uses.

If we go back to the two job opportunities, one pays more while one offers a more flexible schedule. The world may tell us that more money equals more success. However, if we define success as financially and emotionally supporting our family, the lower paying, more flexible job opportunity fits our own authentic definition of success. While the emotional support we provide our families and being present in their lives doesn't come with a paycheck, being there to coach our kids' sports teams and sitting at the family dinner table does provide value.

Yes, taking the higher paying job helps us to keep up with the external world in terms of income, but it does not satisfy our definition of success in this example. Taking the higher paying job in this case would be a defensive move caused by our fear of getting left behind while others around us make more money than us.

In this case, one option would allow us to be successful by our own definition. However, the fear of getting left behind could easily prod us into choosing the alternative that may not be the best fit for our particular needs. We have to be authentic in our decisions and do what is right for us rather than base our decisions on what will help us keep pace with others.

FEAR OF WHAT OTHERS WILL THINK

Concern with what others will think, prevents so many of us from living a satisfying, fulfilling, and happy life. We tend to keep meaning and importance to ourselves. After all, it is personal and part of our true identity. We all to some degree keep our identity to ourselves just below the surface. We protect what has meaning and importance in our lives and even put up a front if we feel our identity could be threatened and face an attack.

Using our personal definition of success to guide the decisions we make might lead us to making decisions that don't look like the ones the rest of the world is making. It can draw attention to ourselves. It can make us appear to be going against the current, which we fear will encourage others to question our decisions. Embracing our "why" takes courage and can make us vulnerable to the outside world.

As a result, so many of us keep our why tucked deep behind the walls we put up to the outside world and pursue meaning and importance in our life privately, part time, as a hobby, or possibly only in our heads in the form of dreaming. Wondering what others will think if we pursue our source of significance can paralyze us. We let the outside world's possible perception of us far outweigh the satisfaction and fulfillment of being ourselves, doing what we love, and sharing what we do.

For many of us, the fear of what others will think is the scariest obstacle we will face in our entire lives. Unfortunately, by "others" we can be talking about as few as five, ten, or twenty people. We are usually talking about people we know and associate with on a regular basis. These are people that we value their opinion, want their respect, and want their approval. It could even be a single person we allow to have too much influence over our happiness.

In a world of eight billion people, we can't let such a small number of people stop us from being the person we want to be and having the life we want to live because we are concerned about what they will think. In many cases, our fears are lying to us. The people we are concerned about are most likely people that only want the best for us. They are our parents, our kids, our friends, our family, and people in our community, and they will most likely support anything we decide to pursue.

There are two ways that we can overcome our fear of what others will think. The first is to find a supportive and encouraging environment to share what we do. We need to find an environment that will help us grow and build our confidence in being ourselves and doing what we love. The second is to fight any negative feedback by throwing ourselves right back into process. Remember, the core of our satisfaction and fulfillment comes from engaging in the process and doing what we love.

Being ourselves and showing our true identity to the outside world can be scary, but we have to overcome the fear of what others will think. There will always be critics and those that don't "get" what we do. However, facing that fear, being ourselves, engaging in what we love to do, and sharing what we do is the path to satisfaction, fulfillment, and happiness in our lives.

COMFORT

Comfort works hand in hand with fear to keep us from living Creative Side Out. Almost every trap we fall victim to on our journey is aimed at our comfort zone. What makes comfort especially dangerous is that it lures us in and tricks us into thinking it is helping us.

We can get lost in our comfort zone. We can lose our drive to grow and get better. We stop working and make no progress on the path of significance. We get in a zone of feeling good enough with our day-to-day lives. We feel safe and we grow complacent, stay where we are, and stop trying to maximize our impact.

It is human nature to want to be comfortable. If we know taking a certain action will be uncomfortable in any way, we would rather not do it. We will even forgo any potential rewards that may result from taking action and choose to settle for less as long as we can stay in our comfort zone.

Fear uses comfort in many ways to prevent us from living the life we are called to live. The most common traps we face are the trap of perfection and the trap of comparison.

TRAP OF PERFECTION

Perfection is the fear of failure and the fear of what others will think working in unison to convince us that we are actually capable of doing what we love free from mistake. Once we can do what we love flawlessly, we can share it with others. No one could possibly think what we love to do is crazy if we can do it perfectly.

This trap convinces us that there is such a thing as perfection and that is what everyone wants to see. However, our imperfections in our creations and our processes are what make them unique and different from any other on the planet. Our imperfections are the source of our value. While our product and our process will never be a perfect fit for everyone, they will be what complements and enhances many people's lives.

Our authentic, unique, and imperfect product and process is a puzzle piece. It fits in this world. Our job is to create that piece and to put it out there into the world for others to find and use. The trap of perfection convinces us that no one will like our product or process, and we will be failures unless we create without flaw. However, the only way we fail is by not engaging and creating at all.

TRAP OF COMPARISON

The trap of comparison plays to our fears of failure and getting left behind. When we think about taking a chance and pursuing what we love, we look ahead to those that have found success on that path. They are so radiant in what they do and how they share. They have found their niche and are supporting their family making a living doing what they love and sharing it. They are where we want to be.

Then we look at where we are on our journey and see how far we have to go to be as good as them. It's easy to get intimidated. Comparison opens the door for us to start thinking about how hard and long the journey ahead really is, and we open the door for our fear of failure to go to work.

We might start thinking about what our lives will be like if we try to do what we love and fail. This triggers us to compare ourselves to those around us who have chosen a more traditional path. What if I try pursuing my interest and fail while everyone else keeps plugging along advancing their careers getting corporate promotions, raises, and bonuses? Now our fear of getting left behind is compounded by our fear of failure.

The trap of comparison can paralyze us before we even take the first step on the path we were meant to walk. We fight this trap not by setting a goal that is too big to accomplish, but by focusing on completing the next task necessary to get us to the next milestone on our journey. We take little steps each day to make progress and we commit to never quitting. Rather than comparing our journey to that of others, we have to compare our journey to where we started. We focus on the progress and the improvement we are making on a micro, day-to-day level, and we adjust our tasks and milestones as needed to help us achieve our goal.

DETOURS

Getting off track

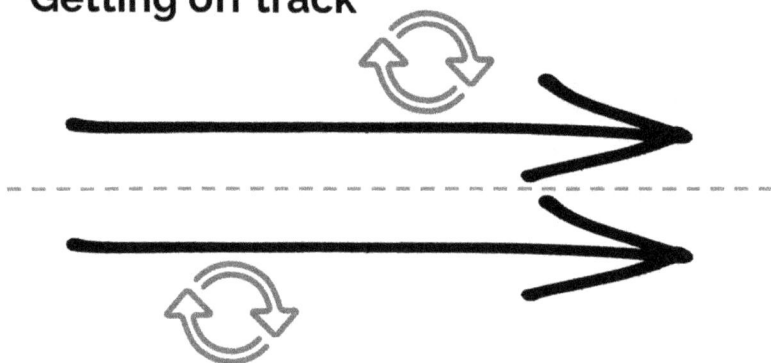

By knowing that fear and comfort are setting traps for us, we can begin to recognize them and be prepared. The more aware we are that they are out there, and the better prepared we are to face them, the fewer times we will take a detour. When we inevitably fall prey to one of their traps, we have the Creative Cycle to get us back on track.

We start with productivity and engage in what we love to do. However, we have another resource at our disposal that can keep us anchored on our path. A resource that we can use as our guide. That resource is authenticity. Being true and honest with ourselves and the world we live in is not always easy, but will keep us living the life we were meant to live.

CREATIVE SIDE OUT HANDBOOK

1. As we strive to merge success and significance into the best life we can live, fear and comfort will always be there to continually try to prevent us from starting and convince us to quit once we are in motion. Fear is the opponent clearly in front of us pushing or holding us back. Comfort is fear in disguise.

2. Fear and comfort each present different traps on our path to live Creative Side Out. Some traps scare us from moving forward while others make it hard for us to leave our current location. The most common traps we face are the trap of perfection and the trap of comparison.

3. We overcome fear and comfort and all of their traps by throwing ourselves into productivity, engaging, and continuing to show up and make progress through repetition. We gain an upper hand on fear and comfort when we use and stick to our own definition of success and find a supporting and encouraging environment to help us grow and share what we do.

DISCOVER & EXPLORE YOUR PATH

1. Brainstorm and identify several potential traps you could fall into that would prevent you from staying on your authentic path. What fears come to mind? What comforts might be holding you back? How could your

journey be uncomfortable? Where will you want to be perfect? How might you be tempted to use "not good enough" as an excuse? Who might you try to compare yourself to? What is the bar you will consistently try to check your work and progress against? Now evaluate and label these traps. Are they designed to keep you from moving forward or make you scared to leave your current position?

2. How will you ensure you don't fall victim to those traps? How will you get back on track if you do find yourself off course? Remember your Creative Cycle. How will you rely on the Creative Cycle and go back to it as a default to overcome the traps of fear and comfort and any other obstacles on your journey?

3. What are the known positives of pursuing your natural interest and curiosity and answering your call by being productive and generous? What are the known positives of not answering your call? Taking only those known positives, which path feels right to you? Which path would provide meaning, importance, satisfaction, and fulfillment in your life? Defer back to this exercise when faced with future decisions that could potentially throw you off track.

MORE TO THE STORY

Getting knocked off my path was tough, but it taught me the most valuable lesson on my journey. I discovered the hard way that there was a third component to living Creative Side Out. It was not only the component that had helped me discover my path in the first place, but it was also the component that was going to guide me back to my path. That third critical component in the Creative Side Out equation was authenticity or simply put, to be myself.

CHAPTER 13

BE YOURSELF

You attract the right things
when you have a sense of who you are.

—Amy Poehler

While productivity and generosity set me in motion, helped me to build momentum, and kept me moving forward in life on a daily basis, they couldn't keep me on the path I had found.

I didn't know it back when success and significance were battling for my time and attention, but authenticity led me to the path I had discovered. The right path. The path I was meant to walk, and the life I was meant to live. Productivity and generosity worked to move me forward and build momentum on the right path, but authenticity is what guided me to the right path in the first place.

Discovering the role of authenticity was a tough lesson, but the most valuable. Authenticity is what helped me find my path. Losing sight of my authenticity allowed me to get off track. Authenticity was the filter I should have been using to make every decision in my life. I now saw it for what it was.

Authenticity was my tool anchoring me to the path I was meant to walk in life. It was my source, my conduit, my compass, and my filter all in one. If I would simply learn how to trust and use it, my authenticity was and always had been the key to navigating life.

Authenticity

Be Yourself

Authenticity is who we are at our core. It is our seed planted on this earth with natural interest, curiosity, ability, and desire. We are all called to discover that seed, water it below the surface through productivity, and give it light above the surface through generosity.

Authenticity is the source of our satisfaction and fulfillment in life. Being who we are is a source of joy and happiness that we can readily tap into by doing what we love and sharing what we do. When we engage and share on a consistent basis we can continue to find satisfaction and fulfillment in our lives.

We often spend so much time trying to cover up who we are and not showing our inner self that it actually prevents us from experiencing what we want most in life if we would simply be ourselves and allow ourselves to pursue what continues to naturally call us.

Authentic discovery and exploration grows us in a child-like manner. Being ourselves, doing what we love, and sharing what we do is our natural adult form of play that adds value to others. When others connect with our work that represents who we are at our core, it highlights the meaning and importance of our lives, and reinforces our connection to our higher power. Being ourselves makes the world a better place, and that is how we find significance.

OUR AUTHENTIC SELF

As young adults we are influenced by TV, movies, and social media without even realizing it. It's easy to get so caught up trying to be like others that we follow and like, that we don't give our authentic self the space it needs to grow.

As adults our daily lives make it easy for us to go with the flow of the everyday current. We have schedules, obligations, commitments, deadlines, and so much noise competing for our attention. It is easy to ignore ourselves. We rarely put ourselves first, and have a tendency to not schedule time dedicated specifically to us.

Living Creative Side Out starts with allowing ourselves the time and space for our true authentic self to be heard. We have to discover our authenticity then experiment with incorporating it into what we do and what we share to find success rooted in significance.

As young adults and adults, we sometimes view that call of our inner voice as something that does not contribute to a task or milestone that will help us achieve our goals and lead us to success in the external world. So, we suppress that inner call. Sometimes we even ignore it, hoping it will go away. As a result, we can be left with that something's missing feeling.

We have to change our mindset. We have to think about the possibility that our inner voice might be calling us to the path that leads to everything we want in life. We have to have the mindset that giving that voice, that call, and our natural interest and curiosity the proper time and attention could be a better path to significance as well as success in our lives.

We live Creative Side Out when we have the mindset that the quiet inner voice in our head and our heart deserves more influence in our lives than the noise in our external world. Then we rely on that voice, our true authentic self, to guide our decisions and keep us on the path in life we are meant to walk. We let who we are define success in our lives, determine what we do, and drive what we share with the world to make our impact and find fulfillment and satisfaction.

AUTHENTICITY AND THE CREATIVE CYCLE

Now that we know that authenticity serves as the third and final component to living Creative Side Out and the Creative Cycle, let's take another look at the Creative Cycle and put it all together.

Authenticity

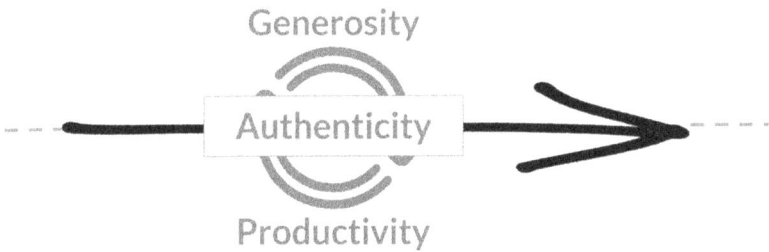

Generosity

Authenticity

Productivity

Productivity: We have to be productive to discover, explore, engage, and grow our authenticity. Productivity is doing the work we are authentically called to do. Productivity is allowing our inner child-like self to play without consequence or fear of failure. It is a process that comes naturally to us and provides us with internal satisfaction and fulfillment.

Generosity: Generosity is the key to not only maximizing the impact of our authenticity in other people's lives, but in our own lives as well. We can be authentic, and even productive, but if we don't share who we are and what we do, we have no chance of having a positive impact in other people's lives. If we don't give ourselves a chance to positively impact others, we don't allow ourselves the opportunity to feel the significance that comes from who we are and what we do.

Generosity is how we let who we are at our very core, who we were created to be, fulfill our purpose and live the life we are meant to live.

IMPLEMENTING AUTHENTICITY

What does it mean to implement our authenticity? How can we truly be ourselves in everything we do? Authenticity balances success and significance in our lives by keeping us anchored in who we are. There are four ways that we can implement our authenticity. It serves as our source, conduit, compass, and filter that guide us to our path and helps us make decisions to keep us anchored on our path.

Authenticity

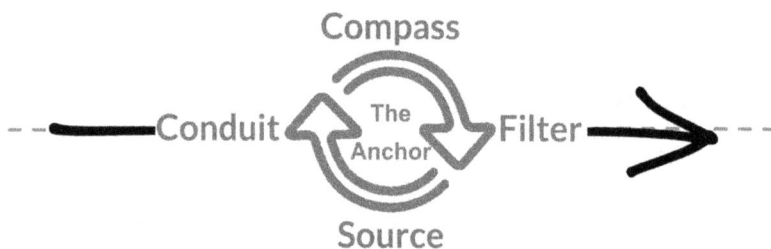

Compass

— — — Conduit   The Anchor   Filter ——→ – – –

Source

OUR SOURCE

The first is to use who we are as our source for satisfaction and fulfillment. We have to talk to ourselves and listen. If we don't, how are we going to know who we are, what is calling us, and what we want out of life? We do this by creating a daily routine or habit that commits us to a certain amount of silence. This gives our inner voice space to talk while we give our full attention and listen.

That voice will call us toward our authentic path in life. That path is our source of fulfillment and satisfaction, and we can consistently tap into that source over and over as long as we take the time to listen to our inner voice and continue to engage in productivity and generosity anchored on our authentic path.

OUR CONDUIT

As we begin to share our work, we have to 100% share what is real and authentic. If we don't, we can come off as being fake or trying to be someone that we are not. Authenticity is what we rely on to take our work that is 100% who we are and put it out there into the external world for others to benefit from. Our internal self that we extract through productivity must pass through this conduit to preserve our authenticity in our work that we share with the external world.

OUR COMPASS

When we give enough time to our inner voice to listen and understand who we are, what we are called to do, and what drives us, the big life decisions are easy to make. Living Creative Side Out draws on our authenticity to help us find the right path in life and use it as our compass to find our authentic path.

Furthermore, when we are faced with a fork in the road or any decision with weight placed on what we choose, we use authenticity as our compass to decide what is right and will keep us on our authentic path we are called to walk. Like a compass, authenticity leads us to our path, helps us stay on that path, and helps us find our way back when we get off track.

OUR FILTER

The final way we implement authenticity in our lives is by using it as our filter to help us process the feedback we receive from the external world. Whether that feedback is good or bad, we filter it against who we are. Sometimes the feedback will ring true and we will makes changes to our process or our product. At other times, the feedback will not resonate with us, and we will appreciate the communication but ultimately move on without implementing any changes.

So, what does that look and sound like? When an opportunity arises, a question is raised, or anyone is trying to sell us on something, we have to ask ourselves does this fit who we are? Does it grow and enhance who we are? Or does it take away from who we are? Does it fit what we love to do? Does it grow our ability and make us better at what we love to do? Or does it distract us from what we are being called to do? Does it help us share who we are? Does it grow our influence and impact we have in the world and on ourselves? Or does it decrease our positive impact on the world and our own lives?

AUTHENTIC GROWTH

As who we are comes into focus, we establish our authentic baseline. We have set a standard that we understand. We know what we are being called toward. We know how to engage our interest and curiosity. We know what value we add to other people's lives as well as our own. Cultivating who we are, what we do, and the impact we have turns into passion.

Passion brings self-discipline, routines, and a commitment to being ourselves, doing what we love, and sharing what we do. However, knowing who we are, having passion, and being disciplined doesn't box us in. It actually allows us to try more things and quickly determine if our new experiences and opportunities are a fit with who we are.

We grow by coloring outside the lines and trying new things. As long as we use our authentic baseline to help us determine if those new things match with who we are, what we do, and the impact we want to have on others, engaging in new things will lead to personal growth.

Our authentic personal growth becomes the force that allows us to keep going and repeat the Creative Cycle over and over. The more we repeat the cycle the easier it becomes for us to transition back and forth from doing what we love to sharing what we do.

Authenticity

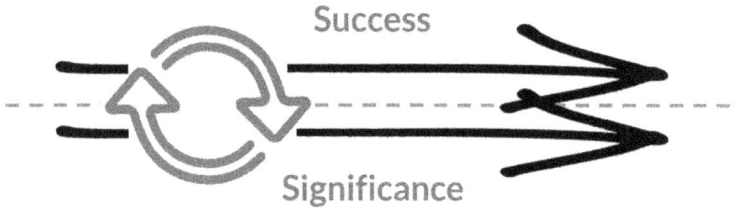

Like a magnet, authenticity forces our internal path of significance and external path of success to draw toward one another creating force and momentum in our lives.

THE AUTHENTIC LIFE

It's hard for others to see significance in who we are. However, the more we are ourselves and add value to our lives and the world around us, the more others begin to sense it. If we are true to who we are, do what we love, and share what we do, then our authenticity can make a positive impact.

People can't help but notice as our authenticity leads us to engaging in what we love to do and we share it. Our passion, impact, and genuine happiness begin to attract others. We begin to experience success rooted in significance.

When we choose to live an authentic life, we shine like a beacon that attracts others. Living an authentic life with the proper balance between productivity and generosity, we begin to radiate and fully live Creative Side Out. People sense our satisfaction, fulfillment, and joy, and they want that in their lives. We begin to inspire and motivate others to live Creative Side Out.

Radiance Zone

Generosity | CSO

Success

Authenticity | Productivity

Significance

What if everyone lived Creative Side Out? What if everyone shined with radiance living the life they are called to live, creating joy in their own lives and the lives of those around them? People would smile more, be more helpful, and inspire others to do the same. We would all be living a life of significance, and the world would be a better place if everyone lived Creative Side Out.

CREATIVE SIDE OUT HANDBOOK

1. Authenticity is who we truly are at our very core. We stay genuine by allowing ourselves the space, time, energy, and attention to explore and express our natural interest, curiosity, ability, and desire.

2. Authenticity anchors us on the path we are called to walk in four ways. It is our source of satisfaction and fulfillment. It is the conduit that allows our internal journey of productivity to flow into the external world. It is the compass that helps us find and stay on the path we are meant to walk in life, and it is the filter we use to process the external response to our work and incorporate it with our productive engagement. Authenticity is the anchor that keeps us balanced between our external journey for success and our internal journey for significance.

3. Knowing who we are, following our passion, and being disciplined doesn't box us in. It actually allows us to try more things and quickly determine if our new experiences and opportunities are a fit with who we are.

DISCOVER & EXPLORE YOUR PATH

1. Create the space to sit in silence and listen to your inner voice for guidance, direction, and your call. Schedule a time and make it a habit. Your inner voice is who you are and your source of authenticity. Keep track of what you hear especially if it keeps telling you something over and over.

2. Does your natural interest, curiosity, ability, and desire take precedence in your decision making? Allow your authenticity to keep you anchored on your true path by using it as your conduit, compass, and filter.

Conduit: Are you being productive and engaging in your natural interest and curiosity? Are you allowing your process and your product to pass through to the external world without modifying it to what you think others want to see and experience? Are you fully allowing your internal productivity and external generosity to communicate, flow, and work together to show the world what has meaning and importance to you?

Compass: What are you being called to pursue? Are you on that path? Have you gotten off that path? How will you know when you are off track? How will you get back on track?

Filter: Allow who you are, what you are being called to pursue, and what has meaning and importance to you to make decisions. Do your goals, uses of time, and practices, add value to who you are, what you do, and how you impact others?

3. How does your authenticity establish your baseline? How can you try new things and measure against your baseline? Does it raise your bar or detract and slow you down lowering your fulfillment, satisfaction, and value created?

MORE TO THE STORY

Even though I had allowed myself to get off track, all was not lost. It was not the end of my creative journey. With the discovery of authenticity's role in living Creative Side Out, I now had all the tools I needed to assess my new reality, find my location, and make the adjustments needed to get back on track.

The first step was being honest with myself and acknowledging once again that the call to write was more than a hobby for me. It required the time, attention, and energy that I had previously created in my life prior to changing companies.

The second step was being honest with my employer. In doing so, we were able to modify my role in the company that benefited us both. Not only did my honesty lead us to create a new position that added tremendous value to the company, but it was one that was more naturally aligned with my personality and skill set.

The change not only put me in a position to better excel at work, but it was a natural fit for me which made work more enjoyably and less stressful. As a result, I instantly became more present during my family time and less exhausted during my writing time. I was starting to get my work-life balance back in check.

I was able to identify where my paths of success and significance were, what they were doing in my life, and re-align them much faster this time. I adapted and started to direct my life back on course toward the path I knew I was being called to walk.

CHAPTER 14

RADIANCE

You have to find what sparks a light in you

so that you in your own way

can illuminate the world.

—Oprah Winfrey

The Creative Side Out formula was complete. I knew all three components: Authenticity, Productivity, and Generosity. The Creative Cycle was that simple. Be yourself, do what you love, and share what you do. I had found my authentic path in life once again. I knew the forces at play in my life and the role of each. I knew if I kept any opposition clearly in front of me, I could face it head on.

No sneak attacks.

I knew exactly what had to be done. I re-established my daily writing habit. As I began to finish songs, I started to share them again. I still didn't have the same amount of time to promote them that I previously had. However, simply playing them for my wife on a Friday night or asking for feedback from members in an online songwriter forum was enough to complete the Creative Cycle and throw me back into productivity. Slowly, I began to create momentum once again.

I made sure to be authentic and honest in everything I was doing and with every decision I was making. I was honest with myself. I accepted that at my very core, I was a writer, and I made writing my focus in life. The process was for me. The songs were for the rest of the world. I protected my writing time at all costs and kept my appointment with myself every day.

I would not give up. I kept showing up every day no matter how small or irrelevant the time may have appeared to be. I allowed my authenticity to guide me toward my source of significance and used meaning and importance to once again define my definition of success. Anchored in authenticity, allowing who I was and what I loved to do to be my source, conduit, compass, and filter. Happiness began to radiate in my life once again.

As the gap between success and significance began to close, living Creative Side Out became a way of life for me. I had proven to myself that living Creative Side Out was how we let our internal authenticity radiate with significance in the external world.

Creative Side Out

Authenticity
(Be Yourself)

Productivity
(Do What You Love)

Generosity
(Share What You Do)

As we make our way around the Creative Cycle more and more, we begin to create synergy in our lives that revolves around who we are at our very core. The more times around the Creative Cycle, the more we embrace, use, grow, and share our natural interest and curiosity. Who we are and what we love to do begins to define our tasks, milestones, and goals in life. We begin to close the gap in our lives between success and significance and gain momentum on the path we are meant to be on in life.

Gain Momentum

LIVE WITH PURPOSE

When we close the gap between success and significance in our lives, we create alignment between who we are and what we do. Answering our call and creating that alignment in our lives provides us with purpose. We begin to live an intentional life that adds value and positively impacts the world. Our internal identity starts to shine in the outside world through our unique process and our genuine product. We begin to live Creative Side Out.

Creative Side Out

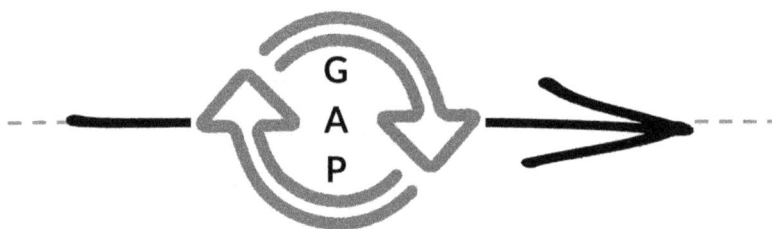

MAKE AN IMPACT

Living Creative Side Out, we embrace who we are. We use and grow our natural interest and curiosity and gain confidence in being ourselves and doing what we love. Staying true to who we are on our authentic path in life, we maximize the value we add to the lives of others as well as ourselves.

The more value we add, the more impact we have. When we positively impact people's lives by being ourselves, doing what we love, and sharing what we do, we begin to radiate. People see that radiance and want it in their own lives. By living Creative Side Out, we encourage and motivate others to discover, embrace, use, grow, and share their authentic journey and inspire others to do the same. The radiance we produce living Creative Side Out can change the world.

Radiance

CREATIVE SIDE OUT HANDBOOK

1. Creative Side Out is an intentional way of living life that allows us to combine the power of success and significance into one magnificent authentic path that radiates and inspires.

2. Through authenticity, productivity, and generosity, we can overcome fear and comfort to find success in our lives rooted in significance maximizing our impact on others as well as ourselves.

3. When we live Creative Side Out, we radiate in the outside world living the life we were meant to live while encouraging and inspiring others to do the same.

DISCOVER & EXPLORE YOUR PATH

1. Think of a time that you encountered someone with radiance. What was the attraction you felt toward that person? How did they draw you in? How did you respond to their radiance? Did you want that in your life? How were you inspired and motivated by them? How can you use your encounter with them to motivate and inspire you to pursue that same radiance in your life?

2. It's time to accept that your calling is who you are at your core. Using the person you identified in the previous question as motivation and inspiration, evaluate the gap between success and significance in your life right now. Think about how closing the gap between success and significance will create alignment between who you are and what you do. You have purpose. You can feel your call. You want and deserve radiance in your life. Take one more look at your tasks, milestones, and goals. Make any adjustments needed and then focus on closing that gap and letting your definition of success become rooted in significance so that you can start living the radiant life that you are meant to live.

3. Drawing inspiration from the person you identified above, write your clean and concise vision of the fu-

ture living Creative Side Out. What will your life be like? What is you ideal life, work, schedule, process, and product look like? Dream big! Now what does your impact look like in your ideal life? How would you hope to impact, inspire, motivate, and positively influence other people's lives? This is the life you are being called to live and are meant to live. That is living Creative Side Out.

MORE TO THE STORY

It didn't take long for me to feel like I was back on the path toward living Creative Side Out. I was back to being myself, doing what I loved, and sharing what I was doing. I was focused on becoming an established writer based on my definition of success, rooted in what had meaning and importance in my life. The radiance I had felt in my life prior to changing companies was resurfacing.

The more I re-established my routine and consistently engaged in my craft, the more confident I became in my writing. My growing confidence helped me expand my impact, reach, and add more value to the world and to my life. I began my transition once again to becoming a successful writer. The goals, milestones, and tasks to get there were no different than before.

However, discovering authenticity and the role it played in my life sent me back to the Creative Cycle with a drive to achieve my goal like never before. I now very clearly saw the path and how to get there. I now fully understood who I was, why I was put on this earth, and how important it was to continue to pursue my authentic call. I learned earlier in my journey that my natural interest and curiosity toward writing was more than a hobby. However, now I knew that writing was without a doubt my gift.

CHAPTER 15
FINDING OUR GIFT

I have no special talents,
I am just passionately curious.

—Albert Einstein

Looking back on my journey I could see how all the pieces fit together. I could clearly see the call to write always being there waiting for me to embrace it. It was a hard emotional road to get to that light bulb moment, but it now all made sense. I could see how it all started with those first two records I used to play as a very small child.

Eventually, my natural interest and curiosity in music led me to playing guitar, seeing live bands, meeting singer-songwriters, and finally giving me a concentration, focus, and a powerful draw toward writing. Looking back, it is easy to see that the draw was always there softly calling me toward it. As I began to hear it, I wasn't sure what it was or the role it played in my life. I explored it, I liked it, I got frustrated with it, I ignored it, I entertained it, and I even walked away from it many times. Yet, it was always there patiently waiting for me to embrace it. The call to write fought the war for my time, energy, and attention because it was more than a hobby. It was my gift.

I think back to how awkward a guitar used to feel in my hands. I think about how hard it was for me to make my fingers not only go to the right places, but to use enough pressure to allow the strings to make the right sound. I couldn't strum. I had no rhythm or sense of timing. My voice was horrible. I couldn't sing worth a lick. Singing and playing guitar at the same time was like trying to jump off of a cliff and fly. I had my mind made up that it wasn't possible, and remembering all of the words to my songs was out of the question. That doesn't sound like a gift.

No wonder I was embarrassed to tell everyone what I was really passionate about. No wonder I kept my writing to myself for so long. It was so incredibly hard for me to dedicate time, energy, and attention to my writing. How could this disaster that was me trying to write songs, play guitar, and sing deserve the same amount of attention as my career and family? Career and family were real. Writing was child's play.

I could now see how far I had come. Yes, it was play and still was, but that's just it. Once I realized that writing was my gift, I realized that it was supposed to feel that way because it was my adult form of play. My gift was that natural interest and curiosity that wouldn't go away. It was my call to keep coming back, engage without consequence of what others would think, use my imagination, create, simply play in a child-like manner, and then show the world what I had created.

As I was growing up and through early adulthood, I knew there were some things I was good at, but I couldn't do anything with such mastery that I would say I was gifted. My journey to find significance and have success opened my eyes to what my gift really was. Discovering how to be authentic, productive, and generous-living Creative Side Out-revealed to me that my gift was not about my natural ability, skill level, and mastery.

My gift was that natural interest and curiosity that wouldn't go away. It was that call that was always there patiently waiting for me to embrace it. It was that unexplainable desire to engage, use, grow, and explore that call. My gift was that raw natural interest and curiosity that I couldn't walk away from.

My gift was not an off-the-charts natural talent that I'd been born with. It was a seed of interest and curiosity that called me to cultivate it. When I allowed myself to embrace, use, grow, and share that seed and its growth, it turned my play into fulfillment and satisfaction for me while adding value to the external world.

FINDING OUR GIFT

Living Creative Side Out means identifying, embracing, growing, and sharing our true purpose. It means using our gift and sharing it with the world so that others can benefit from it. Without a doubt everyone has a creative talent waiting to be found, embraced, grown, and shared with the world. However, we can often overlook our gift because we think of a gift as an extraordinary ability that presents itself as an epiphany of instant mastery.

For the majority of us, our gift subtly calls us over time, and even as we begin to hear the call, we still don't identify it as our gift. Here are a few guidelines to help identify our gift and purpose. If we start to notice something gaining our attention and it checks the majority of these boxes, it very well could be our gift calling us to start living Creative Side Out.

Our Gift

1. Morally and Legally Acceptable

First and foremost, it is important to recognize that our gifts are the inherent good in us that can be embraced, used, grown, and shared to make a positive impact on our lives as well as the lives of others. We are not called to use our gifts in any way that is morally unacceptable or in violation of the law. Talented computer experts are not called to hack bank accounts and steal money. Influential speakers are not called to smooth-talk people into buying goods or services that they know are ineffective and useless just to make a profit. Our gifts are intended to make the world a better place in a moral and legal fashion.

2. Interest NOT Ability

Our gift is more about our level of natural interest, curiosity, and desire than our level of natural ability. This is the biggest misunderstanding about our gift. Many believe that if they do not show a very high level of natural ability at something, then they are not gifted. This is not true.

We are all gifted. Our gift is a call to something. When we answer that call it takes us on a journey and becomes our purpose in life. The gift provides us with satisfaction and fulfillment as we pursue our interest and strive to improve our ability. The interest never goes away, we continue to engage and get better, and eventually others find value in our ability.

3. We Already Engage In Our Gift

We most likely are already aware of our gift, have a natural interest in it, and perhaps are even already pursuing it from time to time or as a hobby. When we look back at our childhood, adolescence, and early adult years we most likely have always been engaging in some facet of using our gift.

If we think about things we engaged in when we were alone or how we entertained ourselves when we were bored, hints of our gift are most likely there. For instance, a world-class drummer might have always been finding random objects and exploring the noise produced from striking them. A songwriter might have always been

222

interested in words that rhyme. An architect may have always wondered what was on the other side of every wall.

4. We Enjoy Our Gift

We enjoy engaging in our gift and look forward to using it. This sounds obvious, but many of us gravitate toward something we enjoy without even thinking much about it. If we have a moment of spare time, instinctively engaging some facet of our gift could be one of the first things that comes to mind as to how we spend that spare time. We may not always actually engage in it, but it is consistently among the options we evaluate. When we do actually engage in this activity, we find that it brings us joy.

5. We Get Lost In Our Gift

We get lost when we engage in our gift, and we lose track of time. Our subconscious takes over. One idea leads to another which then leads us down another line of thought or activity. We explore different thoughts and ideas. We try something new. We go into a free fall of activity. At some point, we probably stop thinking about it all together and just do it. Once we consciously "come to" and need a break, we realize quite a bit of time has gone by.

6. We Are Easily Drawn Into Our Gift

Whether we try to give it up or simply haven't had time to engage our gift in a while, we find that it is not hard to get drawn back into it. Additionally, we are often drawn back to it with more attraction than before. Our purpose will strike a nerve with little effort. Perhaps we see someone else doing it, we read an article about it, or someone simply asks us about it. If our first reaction after being away from it is one of excitement and wanting to pick it back up, that could be an indicator of our gift begging for discovery and space in our lives.

7. Inspired NOT Intimidated

When we encounter professionals or others that are much more advanced at our gift than we are, we are inspired by their ability rather than intimidated. We will find ourselves motivated by their radiance as opposed to thinking we will never be that good. We will want to take note of what they are doing and try to incorporate some of their strategies and tricks of the trade into our own practice. We will feel pushed and want to improve.

Most importantly, we will find ourselves imagining being as good as them, visualizing how that would feel, and starting to figure out the steps we need to take to get there. We may even start to see the possibility of us being just as good if not better than them. A natural confidence, yet humbled attitude, will surface and support our desire to improve and get better when we encounter those farther down the path than us.

8. We Have a Strong Desire to Learn & Teach

We find ourselves wanting to read about others that are pursuing or have pursued a similar gift. Their articles and talks don't bore us. We are fascinated to hear others talk about how they do the same thing and learn techniques they use. We love to hear interviews with other people or professionals that engage and share the craft. We want to read every word in long articles or books on the subject.

We even begin to teach and enlighten others on the subject,

perhaps even to the point of providing them way more on the subject than they care to know! Talking about what we love to do is instinctive. We naturally teach what we know and love which brings a similar satisfaction and fulfillment into our lives to that of engaging in the activity itself. And people will listen and engage us. Experiencing someone's genuine passion about a subject attracts and entertains listeners whether they are passionate about that particular subject or not.

9. People Will See Our Gift in Us

Even when we are an amateur and starting out, others will acknowledge that we are onto something. People will see past our stumbling out of the block, recognize a desire to learn, and genuinely tell us that we are pretty good. Others will encourage us to keep at it. They will inquire about our latest work when they haven't seen us in a while and will have a genuine interest in our progress.

10. We Will Want to Share Our Gift

No doubt, we will be shy and apprehensive, especially as we are starting out and learning, but deep down we will have a strong desire to share what we love doing with others. Out of fear, we will be tempted not to share, but deep inside we will want to know and wonder what others think of our work. The more we produce, and the longer we keep it to ourselves, the more intense our desire to show our work to others will become.

11. Our Gift is Bigger Than Us

Doing and sharing what we love serves others, can improve people's lives, and maybe even change them forever in a positive way.

Our work doesn't have to be big and mainstream to impact or possibly even change other people's lives. However, once we begin to share our work, we realize that our work isn't really about what others think about us as the person that created the finished product. Our work is about how that finished product we created impacts other people.

We will start to notice that it makes them smile. They have a reaction to it. It could be as simple as a story that makes a person who is having a tough day laugh. It could be a product that we make and give someone who really needs it and can't afford it. It could be guidance or instruction that gives a person a new ability, skill, or capacity that they can use to make a better life for themselves and their family. No matter what our product or our process is, when we share it, it adds value to the world and becomes bigger than us.

12. Our Gift Makes Us a Better Person

We are at peace, friendly, happy, and able to give others our full attention when we are routinely engaging our gift. We sleep easy and feel fulfilled after engaging in it. It makes us a better all-around person. Engaging our gift allows us to be better in other areas of our lives. It makes us appealing to interact with. It frees us to give without expecting something in return by either volunteering our services or producing income that we can donate.

By engaging in our authentic call on a regular basis, it's not always on our mind causing us to be distracted as we do other things and engage with other people. Regularly engaging our gift allows us to give other people our full attention when they need it. In contrast, when we fail to use our gift on a regular basis, we become grumpy, moody, difficult to deal with, and don't give everyone and everything our best effort.

13. The Act and Process Satisfies and Fulfills Us

Engaging our gift, the process of actually using and growing it, satisfies and fulfills us more than the finished product itself. We will find that the act of creating or providing a service satisfies us. The more we create and participate, the less impact negative comments about our finished product will have on us. We also won't be as hard on our own work. We will simply move on and throw ourselves into the next project because the process is what we crave and need. Engaging in the activity will always be our response to both praise and negativity because we know that engaging our gift is what satisfies and fulfills us.

Combined, all of these indicators are signs of our gift at work in our lives. We maximize our impact on this world by discovering our gift, and then embracing, using, growing, and sharing it to live Creative Side Out.

JOURNEY NOT DESTINATION

When we honor our call, we discover that life is not about the destination. The journey starts with discovery of our authentic natural interest calling us to play. It culminates over time with our curiosity and desire to use our gift into the core of who we are adding value to the world.

However, that's not where it ends. In fact, there is no end to our journey as long as we live. There is no final destination on this earth. As Julia Cameron says in her book, *The Artist's Way*, "Just when we get there, there disappears." The journey continues to unfold in front of us with each step we take. A little more of the path is revealed and the call continues to naturally draw us farther down the path. We continue to discover more about our gift. We use and grow it more. We add more value, and we ultimately make more of an impact in other people's lives as well as our own.

Significance is what we all truly seek in this life. Significance brings us joy and happiness. Joy and happiness comes from a combination of meaning, importance, satisfaction, and fulfillment. Meaning and importance stem from our authenticity and who we are. Our gift and pursuing our gift with passion and purpose is our true identity. It's always there, and it is our choice to embrace, use, grow, and share it or not.

Our satisfaction and fulfillment comes with persistently answering the call to be ourselves and honor our gift. Like life, satisfaction and fulfillment are not a destination.

When we seek satisfaction and fulfillment through being ourselves, doing what we love, and sharing what we do, we are tapped into our true source of happiness-our gift. Each time we engage in the full Creative Cycle we will find satisfaction and fulfillment. Like success, it will come and go.

When we let significance guide us, we build a body of work. We build on our craft, improve, add value, impact more people, and re-engage our gift. This cycle can be maintained and sustained over the life of our journey by living Creative Side Out.

CREATIVE SIDE OUT HANDBOOK

1. We can often overlook our gift because we think of a gift as an extraordinary ability that presents itself as an epiphany of instant mastery. However, our gift is more about our level of natural interest, curiosity, and desire than our level of natural ability.

2. Discovering, embracing, using, growing, and sharing our gift is our purpose on this earth. Pursuing our call and using our gift feels like play. It is fun, entertaining, satisfying, and fulfilling for us, yet adds value to the world for others to benefit from our gift.

3. Living Creative Side Out means embracing the journey to answer our call and fulfill our purpose. There is no end or final destination. When we pursue our gift, our journey continues to unfold in front of us, revealing a little more of the path, and our call continues to naturally draw us further to discover more about our gift, grow it, and add more value to this world.

DISCOVER & EXPLORE YOUR PATH

1. Use the Creative Side Out Gift Matrix on the following page and identify up to five natural interests that you believe may be your call, your purpose, and your gift in the matrix below. Then check which guidelines apply to each.

2. What did you identify as your gift from the matrix above? How would you rate your current ability to use that gift on a scale of one to ten? How would you rate your current interest, curiosity, and desire to pursue that gift on a scale of one to ten? If your second number is lower than your first, re-evaluate the exercise above. Your interest, curiosity, and passion will always be stronger than your ability even as you become a professional at using your gift.

3. What level of ability from one to ten would you ultimately like to achieve in using that gift? Did you write down a ten? You should have if you have truly identified your gift! However, know that mastering the ability to use your gift cannot peak. There is no final destination. As long as your interest, curiosity, and passion are greater than your ability, your journey will continue to unfold and take you beyond your highest expectations!

Free Download

Creative Side Out Gift Matrix

www.creativesideout.com/csogiftmatrix

Gift & Purpose Matrix
Lists Your Natural Intersts & Check the Guidelines That Apply

creative →

Authenticity (Be Yourself)	Productivity (Do What You Love)	Generosity (Share What You Do)

Natual Interest & Curiosity

Guidelines	1	2	3	4	5
1 Morally & Legally Acceptable					
2 High Interest Despite Ability (Ignore Ability)					
3 Already Engage on Some Level					
4 Enjoy Engaging the Process					
5 Get Lost in Engagement (Lose Track of Time)					
6 Easily Drawn Into Engagement					
7 Inspired (not Intimidated) by Those More Skilled					
8 Strong Desire to Learn & Teach					
9 Others Have Encouraged Pursuit					
10 Desire to Share Process & Product					
11 Serves Higher Purpose (Bigger Than You)					
12 Makes You a Better Person					
13 Process Satisfies & Fulfills You					

Which of Your Natural Interests & Curiosities Checks the Most Boxes? This Could be Your Gift!

Be Yourself | Do What You Love | Share What You Do

MORE TO THE STORY

I felt very fortunate to have discovered my gift of writing. I was grateful that I realized it was there waiting for me to embrace it. The more space I gave it in my life, the better my life became in every aspect. I became more satisfied and fulfilled on a daily basis because I was giving my authentic self the time, energy, and attention it deserved. Allowing myself the first part of my day to engage in play set the tone for me to be my best in other areas of my life for the rest of the day. I became more present with my family and at work by keeping those appointments with myself first thing in the morning.

As I continued to strive to live Creative Side Out day in and day out, one more revelation presented itself. As I walked farther down the path I was called to walk, I realized that I wasn't just a songwriter. I was a writer in general. I started writing about my experiences. I wrote this book. I started several fiction novels. And of course, I continued to write songs.

Writing songs was simply how my authentic call first presented itself. Music was the trail-head to the life I was meant to live and the path I was being called to walk. I not only discovered that I was more than a songwriter, I also revealed to myself that at my very core, I wasn't just a writer. I was a storyteller. It's easy to see now looking back. I had always been a storyteller.

The fact that you are reading this book means that I completed significant tasks, achieved milestones, and met goals on my journey. I created an outward sign of success that everyone can see: this book. What matters most is that my success was rooted in personal meaning and importance. I am one step farther on my authentic path. I found satisfaction and fulfillment by engaging in storytelling, which is what I love to do. I told my authentic story, and I shared it with the world. I succeeded in the external world and found internal significance all while remaining true to who I am.

I will continue to live and teach the Creative Side Out way of life. It is my hope that my journey to be myself, do what I love, and share what I do has encouraged and motivated you to find and walk your own authentic path in life. In doing so, I know you will inspire others to do the same.

FINAL THOUGHTS
CHANGING THE WORLD

Be what you are. Do what you love. Speak what you feel. Don't hide your humanity. Celebrate it. Embrace it. That is how you change the world.

—Vironika Tugaleva

To live Creative Side Out is to find that one authentic path in life we were born to walk and take it. It's having the courage to embrace that path, walk it, grow from it, and share our journey with the world. It's allowing our authenticity to serve as our source, conduit, compass, and filter anchoring us on our true path in life. It's creating daily habits that maximize our productivity and growth. It's being generous with our product and our process so that who we are and the life we live adds value to the world.

We all explore our natural interest and curiosity without consequence as children. However, at some point we become aware of the external world around us and grow self-conscious and even afraid to be ourselves. In our journey to find where we fit in, we often hold back who we are and what we are naturally drawn toward. For some, we hold back so much that we begin to lose our unique identity. We become driven and motivated to have the same success that we see those around us experiencing to the point of living an unauthentic life that leaves us with a void despite the achievements we accomplish.

Significance is what we all truly seek. We want to know that our lives have meaning and importance. We want to find fulfillment and satisfaction in what we do and the impact we have. There is only one path to significance, and it's anchored in authenticity. We have to stay true to who we are and not only hold on to our own unique identity, but give it space to grow and impact our lives and the lives of others.

We have to define success for ourselves rooted in our natural interest and curiosity because that is our gift. When we answer the call to embrace, use, and grow our gift, we allow ourselves to engage in play without consequence, and we find fulfillment and satisfaction. When we choose to share our product and our process, we allow our internal natural gift to add value into the external world. Our authenticity then provides meaning and importance to us in our everyday lives. The more we engage and share our gift the more we radiate, the more people we impact, and the more significant our life becomes living Creative Side Out.

Knowing and understanding the roles that success and significance play in our lives, we can allow them to work in unison to live the life we were meant to live. Knowing and understanding that we will encounter fear and comfort on our journey, we can live Creative Side Out to overcome them by simply being ourselves, doing what we love, and sharing what we do.

We are called to be authentic, productive, and generous with our gifts by our higher power. The beauty of simply being ourselves, doing what we love, and sharing what we do is that it provides us with the internal satisfaction, importance, and meaning we all seek in life while at the same time adding value to the external world. Living Creative Side Out leads us to success rooted in significance.

Whether we decide to transition our lives to using our gifts full-time or not, we are all called to make them a priority in our lives on a regular basis. In doing so, we will live the life we were meant to live and inspire and motivate others to do the same. No matter how small or insignificant our natural interest and curiosity may seem, it is how we as unique individuals impact and change the world.

Changing the World

My deepest hope is that my story about living Creative Side Out has inspired and motivated you to find and pursue your own authentic path in life. In turn, I hope that your authentic journey motivates and inspires others to do the same. Living Creative Side Out is a teachable way of life. To say that someone is living "Creative Side Out" is to say that they are undeniably living the life that they were meant to live and maximizing their positive impact on the world. Being ourselves, doing what we love, and sharing what we do adds peace, harmony, and beauty to the world. Collectively, the more people we inspire to live Creative Side Out, the more beautiful the world becomes.

FOR YOUR JOURNEY
MY GIFT TO YOU

Be sure to grab the complimentary *Creative Side Out Handbook* designed to serve as a quick reference guide to help you start living Creative Side Out on the path you were meant to walk in life:

creativesideout.com/csohandbook

You can connect with me personally on Twitter and Instagram @thestevesample. Thank you for allowing me the opportunity to be a part of your journey in life. I look forward to connecting and experiencing your radiance from living Creative Side Out soon!

LIVING CREATIVE SIDE OUT
AUTHOR NOTES

As I began to discover that writing was more than a hobby in my life, I simply started pulling a thread that was always there with no idea where it would lead. I never would have guessed that I was going to discover a new way of life that provided satisfaction, fulfillment, and happiness.

I implemented changes in my life to make writing a priority. I restructured my mindset, my environment, and my habits to focus on what meant the most to me. I started making decisions and setting goals rooted in significance. In doing so, I found satisfaction and fulfillment in even the smallest increments of progress while building momentum toward writing success.

As my quality of life began to change, I knew this self-reflection and revelation was something I wanted my kids to know. This book started as a few short notes and ideas on life for them to read as they got older. It turned into 50,000 words of unorganized and disconnected thoughts. It was a mess, made no sense, and quite honestly was boring.

However, just like my songwriting, I felt a natural interest and call to keep refining my thoughts. I am a visual person. So, to help me understand what I was trying to say, I drew pictures. Those illustrations not only helped me better understand the forces at work in my life, but helped me clarify my message and became a part of the book as a way for me to help explain how to navigate those forces in life. This was starting to make sense.

To make a long story short, I rewrote the entire book after my first draft, edited it three more times after that, and have read this manuscript over two dozen times in creating the book you hold in your hand right now. During the year it took me from first word to published book, I thought about quitting so many times.

Every time I stopped writing and walked away from this book, I thought writing it was a dumb idea. Who was going to read it? Does it even make sense? What will others think? Fear was always there tempting me to quit. In fact, it's sitting on my desk right now looking back at me. It's whispering in my ear that it's not too late to save myself from this embarrassment. No one has to read this. I don't have to share my authenticity. There is still time to keep hiding and save myself from what others will think about me, my writing, and my journey.

However, every time I returned to this book, picked up my work, and read it again, the call and my desire to share what I have written has grown even stronger. I truly believe that this book will improve people's lives. I believe the more people that live Creative Side Out, the better and more beautiful our world will become.

I started this journey awkward and unsure of what I was doing. I finish this book as a songwriter, author, and storyteller that is a little more skilled and confident as I continue to walk the path I know I am meant to walk in life.

I have grown from writing this book. I hope you have grown from reading it. I'd love to hear your thoughts. Please send me an email, let me know what you think, and let's discuss your journey to be yourself, do what you love, and share what you do living Creative Side Out.

steve@thestevesample.com

Good luck on your journey.

Thanks for being a part of mine.

—Steve

IF THIS BOOK WAS HELPFUL...
QUICK FAVOR

First of all, thank you for allowing me the opportunity to be a part of your journey in life. My deepest hope is that my story to live Creative Side Out has inspired and motivated you to find and pursue your own authentic path in life which in turn inspires and motivates others to do the same.

SO, I HAVE TO ASK ... DID YOU ENJOY THIS BOOK?

If you feel inspired, motivated, and enjoyed this book, would you please take a moment to leave an honest review for *Creative Side Out*? Reviews are the BEST way to help others purchase the book and the first step you can take to ensure that others are inspired and motivated to live Creative Side Out.

You can go to the link below and write your thoughts. I really appreciate you, and thank you again for allowing me to be a part of your journey!

creativesideout.com/csobookreview

IT TAKES A TEAM
GRATITUDE

To my wife and best friend, Michelle. This book would not have been possible without your sacrifice and encouragement. Our souls have always connected on a level that, in good times or bad, all we ever needed were two chairs and a drink. May we never stop changing the view from those two chairs. Thank you for sharing this journey with me. I love you.

To my boys, Cade, Blake, and Owen. If no one else in the entire world reads this book other than three of you, then my goal in writing it has been accomplished. You guys will never know the joy you bring into my life. I am honored to be your dad, and only want one thing for each of you. My deepest hope is that you never lose your child-like love for life. Don't ever let anyone talk you off of your authentic paths in life. May you always be yourself, do what you love, and share what you do. Then inspire and motivate others to do the same. In doing so, you all will have lived your lives to the fullest while leaving behind a world better than the one you were born into. Love you! Too much!

To my mom, dad, brother, and all of my friends and family that are too numerous to name. Thank you for encouraging and supporting my journey to write and tell stories. At times, it must have looked like a disaster from the outside looking in, but none of you ever tried to caution me about continuing down this path. You all saw the radiance within me before anyone else including myself. Thank you!

To my book team: I owe so much to Honorée Corder for her guidance and mentoring as my book coach; Alyssa Archer for going above and beyond with her edits and suggestions; Amy Teegan for proofreading and polishing, Dino Marino for incredible formatting work and cover design, and Kevin Tumlinson for taking time from his own successful author pursuits to provide copy writing expertise. All of your combined efforts make me shine as an author. I am forever grateful for your ideas, input, and hard work. Thank you! Special thanks to Victoria S. Carlson (leadershiphooligans.com), Athena Laz (athenalaz.com), and Vironika Tugaleva (vironika.org) for allowing me to share some of their words of wisdom. You all are truly living life Creative Side Out. Thank you!

Lastly, to my book launch team: I wish I could name you all personally, but that would be a book in and of itself! I am forever grateful for your support and help in making this book a success and helping to inspire and motivate others to live Creative Side Out!

STEVE SAMPLE
ABOUT THE AUTHOR

Steve Sample was born and raised in Beaumont, Texas. During his sophomore year at Monsignor Kelly Catholic High School, he bought a used Sears & Roebuck guitar from a friend for twenty-five bucks.

As it turned out, his friend didn't own a guitar. In the end, Steve's friend was awarded a five dollar commission, his friend's brother (the rightful owner) swept the rest, and Steve kept the guitar.

He attended Texas A&M University where he struggled to learn cover songs on that same cheap guitar. So, one night he decided to write an original song. A fire was lit and a hobby soon turned into passion.

Several years after graduating Fightin' Texas Aggie Class of

2000, he discovered Music City. Today, he continues to make frequent trips to Nashville with two simple goals: Write the next song better than the last, and to meet, connect, and write with other writers that share the passion to impact people through words and music.

Steve believes that everything we want in life can be found by being ourselves, doing what we love, and sharing what we do. Living Creative Side Out, he hopes that others will find inspiration and motivation to discover and pursue their own authentic path in life.

Steve lives in The Woodlands, Texas with his wife, Michelle, and their three boys, Cade, Blake, and Owen. He wakes up at 4:40 A.M. every morning to steal two hours to write before the day erupts into the beautiful chaos that is life. He is a songwriter. He is an author. He is a storyteller.

As for that cheap guitar ... while it survived a shady business transaction and college life, it was no match for a two-year-old. It now hangs in disrepair in Steve's home studio surrounded by other guitars that literally cost 100 times more than he paid for that first one. It may not have any songs left in it, but Steve is forever grateful to that cheap guitar for leading him to the rich path he was meant to walk living Creative Side Out.

Steve Sample Creative, LLC

steve@thestevesample.com

http://www.thestevesample.com

Twitter & Instagram: @thestevesample

Facebook: http://www.facebook.com/thestevesample

www.ingramcontent.com/pod-product-compliance
Lightning Source LLC
LaVergne TN
LVHW041218080426
835508LV00011B/987